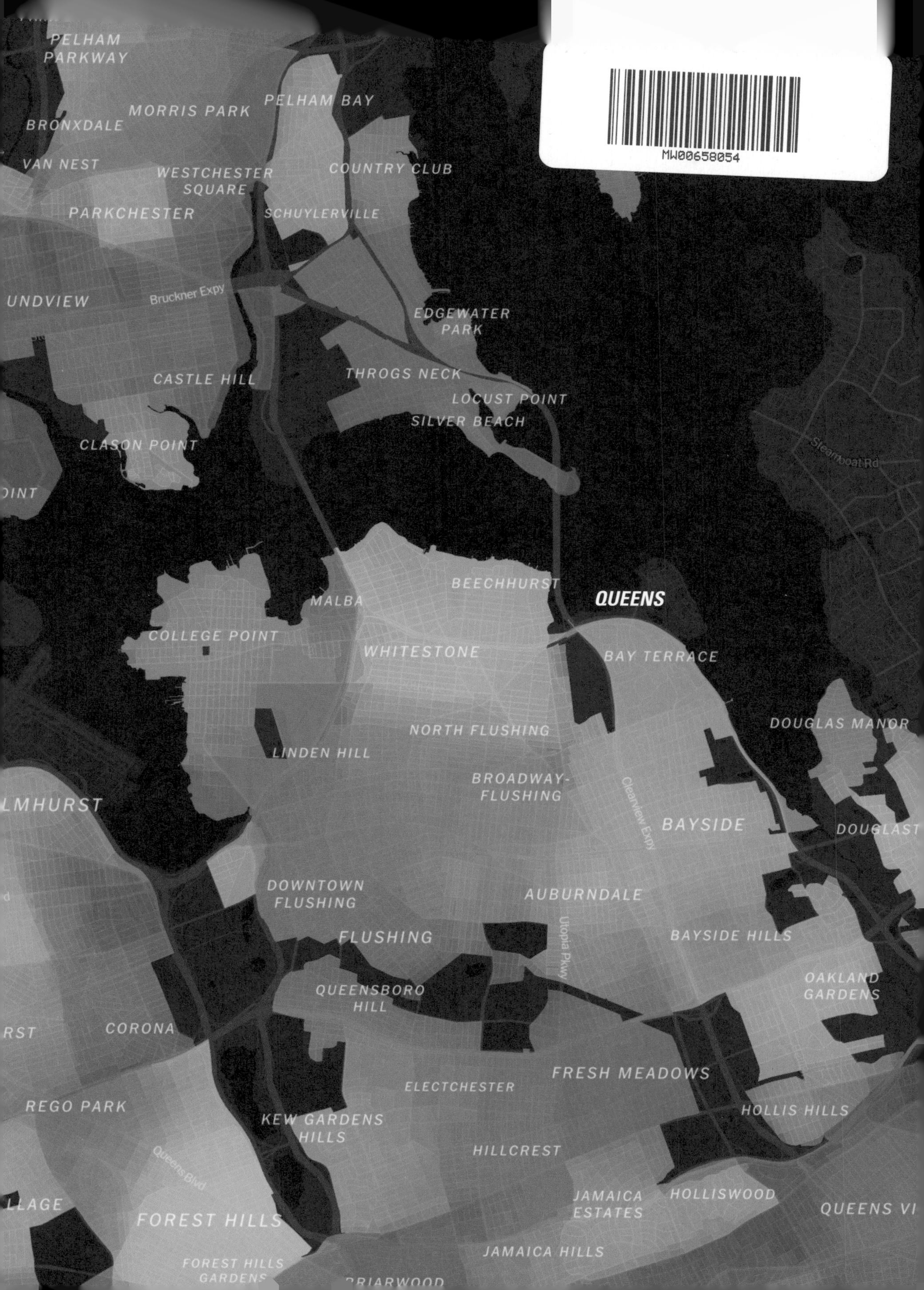
PELHAM PARKWAY
MORRIS PARK
PELHAM BAY
BRONXDALE
VAN NEST
WESTCHESTER SQUARE
COUNTRY CLUB
PARKCHESTER
SCHUYLERVILLE
Bruckner Expy
EDGEWATER PARK
CASTLE HILL
THROGS NECK
LOCUST POINT
SILVER BEACH
CLASON POINT
Steamboat Rd
BEECHHURST
QUEENS
MALBA
COLLEGE POINT
WHITESTONE
BAY TERRACE
DOUGLAS MANOR
NORTH FLUSHING
LINDEN HILL
BROADWAY-FLUSHING
Clearview Expy
BAYSIDE
DOWNTOWN FLUSHING
AUBURNDALE
Utopia Pkwy
FLUSHING
BAYSIDE HILLS
QUEENSBORO HILL
OAKLAND GARDENS
CORONA
FRESH MEADOWS
ELECTCHESTER
REGO PARK
KEW GARDENS HILLS
HOLLIS HILLS
HILLCREST
Queens Blvd
JAMAICA ESTATES
HOLLISWOOD
FOREST HILLS
JAMAICA HILLS
FOREST HILLS GARDENS

A NOTE FROM THE MAPMAKER
by Larry Buchanan

"You start building your private New York," the author Colson Whitehead writes, "the first time you lay eyes on it."

I began building mine in my first New York neighborhood, in Brownstone Brooklyn, on the edge of a toxic canal, right on the corner where Jimmy nearly whacks Karen in that scene from *Goodfellas*. Most people call it Carroll Gardens. Tommy, the old guy who kept watch on my old block, called it South Brooklyn. Depending on which side of Smith Street you're on, you could make an argument that it's Gowanus.

Over time, I became fascinated with these blobs of blurry blocks, one neighborhood bleeding into the next.

Neighborhoods are possibly our most useful, and most nebulous, units of geography. No matter how certain you are that your neighborhood definitely starts here and ends somewhere, there is actually no way to check, no one source for all New York City neighborhood borders. On maps their names are always placed above blocks, unbounded and unbordered, simply floating in cartographic space. The borders on Google Maps are not official. StreetEasy's definition of Prospect Heights is different from Douglas Elliman's.

New York's grid stays the same, but its map is always changing. That's how Yellow Hook becomes Bay Ridge, Tubby Hook becomes Inwood, and Red Hook stays Red Hook. And Hallet's Cove becomes Astoria. And Lispenard's Meadows and the Cast Iron District and Hell's Hundred Acres become some mush of SoHo, TriBeCa, and Hudson Square. And Hudson Yards appears. And Little Italy shrinks as the neighborhood named for north of it grows. And Chinatown holds on.

The only real way to really know where New York City's neighborhoods start and end is for the people who live in them to tell you. So, last year, a few of my colleagues and I created a project at *The New York Times*. We asked New Yorkers to help us map our city, to name and draw the borders of their neighborhoods, to reveal part of their private New York. Nearly 50,000 people responded. The map on the jacket and end pages of this book is the result.

"There are eight million naked cities in this naked city," Whitehead writes. "They dispute and disagree." Pile those 50,000 overlapping shapes on top of each other, across tens of thousands of city blocks, and those disputes and disagreements become visible. You can see the blurry borders where gentrification battles are playing out. You can see the sharp borders, too, that are preserved by history and highways, environment and ego. You see blocks where new "littles"—Little Yemen, Little Bangladesh, Little Caracas—are taking hold and the blocks where old littles were are fading. Areas with rich, pure colors signal strong agreement on what people call these blocks. Areas where the colors blend or get muddy suggest less agreement.

We made this map with love for the city. We all care about it: what it is now, what it once was, and what it will be in the future. The map has a little flavor of all three. So take a close look and remember, next time you get in a fight about what you call where you live, you're right.

But they are, too.

BEYOND ARCHITECTURE: THE NEW NEW YORK

BEYOND ARCHITECTURE:
THE NEW NEW YORK

Barbaralee Diamonstein-Spielvogel, Editor

Vishaan Chakrabarti
Justin Davidson
Andrew Dolkart
Thomas Dyja
Paul Goldberger
Adam Gopnik
Michael Kimmelman
Guy Nordenson
Nat Oppenheimer
A.O. Scott
Lisa Switkin
Rosemary Vietor

NEW YORK REVIEW BOOKS

New York

THIS IS A NEW YORK REVIEW BOOK
PUBLISHED BY THE NEW YORK REVIEW OF BOOKS
207 East 32nd Street, New York, NY 10016
www.nyrb.com

FIRST EDITION

Library of Congress Cataloguing-in-Publication Data

Names: Diamonstein-Spielvogel, Barbaralee, Editor.
Title: Beyond architecture : the new New York / Editor, Barbaralee
  Diamonstein-Spielvogel ; with essays by Vishaan Chakrabarti, Justin
  Davidson, Andrew Dolkart, Thomas Dyja, Paul Goldberger, Adam Gopnik,
  Michael Kimmelman, Guy Nordenson, Nat Oppenheimer, A.O. Scott, Lisa
  Switkin, Rosemary Vietor.
Other titles: Beyond architecture (New York Review Books (Publisher))
Description: New York : New York Review Books, [2025] | Includes
  bibliographical references.
Identifiers: LCCN 2024028630 (print) | LCCN 2024028631 (ebook) | ISBN
  9781681379104 (hardcover) | ISBN 9781681379111 (ebook)
Classification: LCC NA108.N48 B49 2025 (print) | LCC NA108.N48 (ebook) |
  DDC 720.9747/1—dc23/eng/20240722
LC record available at <https://lccn.loc.gov/2024028630>https://lccn.loc
  .gov/2024028630
LC ebook record available at <https://lccn.loc.gov/2024028631>https://lccn.loc
  .gov/2024028631

ISBN 978-1-68137-910-4
Available as an electronic book; ISBN 978-1-68137-911-1

Printed in the United States of America.
10 9 8 7 6 5 4 3 2 1

To the collaborative efforts of the women and men who occupy, rescue, restore, recycle, and preserve our architectural heritage, and contribute their time, thought, energy, and money to the preservation of the landmarks of New York.

CONTENTS

One of the finest examples of the City Beautiful movement, the David N. Dinkins Municipal Building (1909–1913) includes the 20-foot-tall figure of *Civic Fame*. PHOTO: ZACK DEZON.

BEYOND ARCHITECTURE:
THE NEW NEW YORK

The 20-foot-tall figure of *Civic Fame*, atop the David N. Dinkins Municipal Building (1909–1913), stands perched on a globe. She holds a shield with the New York City coat of arms; a laurel branch symbolizes victory. The crown with dolphins represents the city's relationship to the sea, and its five crenellations represent the then-recent 1898 unification of the five boroughs into one metropolis. PHOTO: ALAMY.

BARBARALEE DIAMONSTEIN-SPIELVOGEL

THE ROAD WE TRAVELED BY …

FOR EVERY DECADE SINCE 1980, and occasionally in between, we have celebrated the anniversary of the New York City Landmarks Law, the agency it created, and its impact on New York City, and have worked to stimulate communal engagement, community activism, and collaboration. Such dedication, on my part, to the cause of historic and cultural preservation began even earlier. As a child, I lived for some years in a town founded in 1752, whose Main Street, the historic center of the Lehigh Valley, was often referred to as the finest Victorian Main Street in the United States.

While I lived in Charlottesville, Virginia,[1] and, later, in the Tidewater area, my understanding was enhanced by the atmosphere, lifestyle, and traditions of the South. Nearby Tidewater is Colonial Williamsburg,[2]

---

1   Charlottesville is so steeped in history and so admiring of the genius of Thomas Jefferson (generally referred to by all as "TJ") that, up until 2019, the former president's birthday was celebrated as an official city holiday. Jefferson's architectural achievements included the founding and construction of the University of Virginia, a centerpiece of Charlottesville, and the construction of nearby Monticello, his neoclassical house, replete with countless inventions indicating his talents, worldliness, and creative genius. Together, they form a UNESCO World Heritage Site. For more information, see UNESCO World Heritage Convention, https://whc.unesco.org/en/list/442/ (accessed April 4, 2024).

2   The restoration of Williamsburg's historic district and the creation of Colonial Williamsburg, a 301-acre historic area and living history museum, began in 1926. It includes several hundred restored or recreated eighteenth-century buildings, alongside seventeenth-century, nineteenth-century, and Colonial Revival structures. In 1932, the first exhibition building opened to the public: a twentieth-century reconstruction of the Raleigh Tavern, a historic building where members of Virginia's House of Burgesses, the first democratically elected legislature in the colonies, met after the body was dissolved by the English governor before the American Revolution.

which today still provides an evocation of history through its eighty-nine original eighteenth-century buildings and hundreds of reconstructions; Savannah, founded in 1733 as the first planned neoclassical city in the United States and understandably proud of its past;[3] and Charleston, founded in 1670 and home of the South Carolina Historical Society, established in 1855 to preserve the state's rich historical legacy. Extensive travels and living abroad also fostered my interest in studying and preserving our own intriguing and peculiarly American histories.

These earlier experiences led me to welcome my responsibilities as a member of the Landmarks Preservation Commission (LPC). As the longest-serving member of the commission (1972–1987, during four mayoral administrations), I organized the first anniversary event in 1980. We drew upon my book *Buildings Reborn: New Uses, Old Places* (1978), one of the earliest examinations of "adaptive reuse," a phrase used in the book frequently and, we believe, created

---

3 Savannah, Georgia, was the first planned city in the United States. Its elegant and complex layout included public squares, neoclassical architecture, and a substantial road system that encouraged the growth of urban markets. Historic Savannah Foundation was established in 1955 as an early preservation organization that, by 1962, had created a comprehensive inventory of the city's 1,100 historic structures. See Beth Reiter, "Historic Savannah Foundation," in *New Georgia Encyclopedia*, last modified May 4, 2021, at https://www.georgiaencyclopedia.org/articles/arts-culture/historic -savannah-foundation/ (accessed March 26, 2024).

by architect Giorgio Cavaglieri, whose work included the restoration of the Jefferson Market Library (formerly the Jefferson Market Courthouse) and the Public Theater (formerly the Astor Library and the Hebrew Immigrant Aid Society). As part of that 15th Anniversary commemoration, installations of large-scale green-and-white banners with the words "Buildings Reborn" were placed on the façades of "reborn historic buildings" throughout the five boroughs to engage, inform, and educate wider numbers of passersby about the meaning and practices of historic preservation. The aim of these installations was to transform general ideas of preservation and reuse into a comprehensible, purposeful, and less remote and esoteric practice.

During my first years as a member of the Landmarks Preservation Commission,[4] the necessity for outreach and education became clear.[5] My intent was to encourage the response of committed and devoted community supporters and to engage broad numbers of the public who, though often unaware, were affected by its actions. The work of the commission evolved when the Landmarks Law was extended in 1973, and enabled in 1974, to include scenic landmarks and interiors. This expanded mandate, coupled with newly regularized hearing schedules, generated even more frequent meetings and designation

---

4 Early in Diamonstein-Spielvogel's service, Landmarks Preservation commissioners spent endless uncounted hours reviewing violations at commission meetings. The most common and frequent explanation offered by property owners for violations was that they were unaware they lived within a historic district or within a designated building. From 1987 to 1995, when Diamonstein-Spielvogel was chair of the Landmarks Preservation Foundation, it became evident that there was no manifest indication of the existence of historic districts in New York City.

5 In response to the need for outreach and education, Diamonstein-Spielvogel created and developed several signage programs: the Historic District Maps and Marker Program (1988) and the Historic District Street Name Signs Program (1989) aided in identifying all designated districts. As chair of the Historic Landmarks Preservation Center, she established the Cultural Medallions Program (1995) to commemorate notable New Yorkers throughout the five boroughs with medallions placed on existing historic buildings where they had lived or worked. To date, 145 medallions have been installed. Because the building must still exist, and the property owner must agree, HLPC has been unable to honor all appropriate nominees. For example, Walt Whitman, George Balanchine, and Duke Ellington were not honored, as the owners of those buildings would not grant permission, nor Shirley Chisholm, as her home in Brooklyn no longer exists. Diamonstein-Spielvogel also commissioned the distinctive black-and-white terra-cotta Historic District Markers, Historic District Street Name Signs, and oval Cultural Medallions, which were all designed pro bono, from internationally renowned graphic designer Massimo Vignelli. As a founding member of the Landmarks Conservancy Board, Diamonstein-Spielvogel also created the Living Landmarks Award, which proved to be one of the more successful fundraising awards in the preservation community. The establishment of these programs helped provide visual shape, form, and identity to the work of preservation.

hearings.[6] By August 2024, the designation of 157 historic districts and extensions, 1,464 individual landmarks, 123 interior landmarks, and 12 scenic landmarks has given the Landmarks Preservation Commission oversight responsibility for more than 38,000 structures throughout the five boroughs—a significant task for what is one of the city's smallest agencies,[7] yet considered one of the most influential preservation agencies in the United States.

The increase in oversight responsibility pushed the agency to streamline its processes and standardize its review procedures. The commission established master plans for specific areas and published online guides to enhance its accessibility to the average applicant. Decisions once made by the full commission are currently decided by staff, using recently approved agency guidelines.[8] And as of 2023, applications are filed through an online portal entitled Portico,[9] which incorporates the agency's expedited review services.

The long-term impact of these commendable efforts to streamline the review process—whether beneficial or deleterious—remains to be seen. While in favor of the accelerated process, critics have raised justifiable concerns about

---

6   This addition to the law was in large part due to the ongoing, behind-the-scenes support of Deputy Mayor Richard R. Aurelio, who served during the Lindsay administration. From its beginning, Aurelio saw the merits and importance of landmark designation and quietly helped move forward the expansion of this mandate to include scenic landmarks. The amendments to the Landmarks Law, which passed in November 1973, and went into effect in 1974, established that interior and scenic sites could be designated landmarks if they were at least thirty years old and possessed "a special character or special or aesthetic interest." Interior landmarks, with the exception of spaces used for religious worship, are required to be open and accessible to the public. The amendments further strengthened the commission's role by regularizing its scheduled meetings; the Real Estate Board spoke against the amendments, which passed the city council by a vote of 36 to one, with one abstention.

7   Although one of the smallest New York City agencies, composed of eleven commissioners and eighty staff members, the New York City Landmarks Preservation Commission is the largest preservation agency in the United States, and the bellwether of our nation.

8   Sweeping changes to agency rules were proposed in 2018. The New Rules Initiative was a 131-page proposal to reduce the number of public hearings, expedite applications by reclassifying them to be subject to only staff-level review, and reduce the time allotted for review by the agency. Owing to pushback from the preservation community, these proposals were eventually modified and adopted in a more limited form in 2019; see Craig Hubert, "Public Mostly in Favor of Revised LPC Rules Changes, But Think More Work Can Still Be Done," *Brownstoner*, October 17, 2018, https://www.brownstoner.com/architecture/landmarks-preservation-commission-rules-changes-second-public-hearing/ (accessed March 22, 2024).

9   The new portal can be reached at https://www.nyc.gov/site/lpc/applications/apply.page (accessed March 22, 2024).

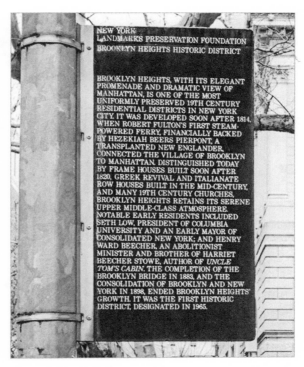

Two signage programs, the Historic Districts Street name sign (1989) and the Historic Districts Maps and Markers (1988), were created by Barbaralee Diamonstein-Spielvogel to inform the public about historic district boundaries. Both were designed pro bono by Massimo Vignelli.

the diminished involvement of commissioners in the final review.[10] Certainly, existing agency protocols previously allowed solely internal reviews. One example is the Certificate of No Effect, a staff-level review supervised only by the chair and set apart from public input. In addition, rules continue to permit modified applications that have already been heard at a public meeting to bypass additional public hearings. While interested parties may submit materials in writing, this procedure could cause an erosion of public discourse and oversight. Concerns about this shift, and the subsequent increase in decision-making powers delegated to the chair, have been raised. These responsibilities are possibly too taxing for any single individual.[11] Additionally, the use of staff-level reviews for potentially significant design changes

---

10 See Christabel Gough, *Regulatory Capture: Watching a City Commission Lose Its Way* (New York: A Report from the Society for the Architecture of the City, 2023), 6–7, 9.

11 Some critics have argued that the agency has retreated in the face of real estate interests, citing the various lawsuits brought against the Landmarks Preservation Commission, not by the regulated real estate industry but by preservationists, because of the agency's failure to designate. Ibid., 3.

Edith Wharton
1862-1937

14 West 23rd Street
Manhattan

This was the childhood home of Edith Jones Wharton, one of America's most important authors, at a time when 23rd Street marked the northern boundary of fashionable New York. Here, in her father's extensive library, young Edith Jones discovered the world of literature. Wharton wrote with authority on gardens and design, but was most celebrated for her fiction. Her novels and stories are characterized by her intelligence, perception and the great beauty of her prose. She revealed the life of the soul with courage and clarity. Wharton lived in France for the latter part of her life, but the complex world of patrician New York remained the source of her greatest fiction. This includes *The House of Mirth* (1905) and *The Age of Innocence*, for which, in 1921, she became the first woman to win the Pulitzer Prize for Literature.

The Historic Landmarks
Preservation Center
October 5, 2011

PLAQUE PROGRAM CONCEIVED BY BARBARALEE DIAMONSTEIN-SPIELVOGEL

The Cultural Medallion program of the Historic Landmarks Preservation Center commemorates the lives and work of notable New Yorkers. In 1995, its creator Barbaralee Diamonstein-Spielvogel commissioned international designer Massimo Vignelli to design the New York City Landmarks Preservation Commission–approved medallion. As of 2025, 145 medallions have been installed throughout the five boroughs.

could result in questionable outcomes,[12] restrict public discourse, and reduce the agency's effective execution of its mandate, if the pursuit of swift customer service overtakes the agency's commitment to maintaining historic properties by law.

As the agency has evolved, our strong commitment to, and citizen participation in, the processes of the Landmarks Preservation Commission have continued. For the 50th Anniversary commemoration in 2015, an Alliance of nearly 190 organizations was formed to stimulate the understanding, appreciation, and interest of a wider public concerning the Landmarks Law and its future role in preserving and enhancing the quality of life for New Yorkers and visitors alike.[13] Now, a decade later, with the 60th Anniversary, the goals of public involvement, collaboration, connectivity, and awareness, which were fundamental to the formation of the Alliance, continue.

The years since 2020 have been catalytic for New York City in ways that

12 See, for example, the discussion of the McGraw-Hill interior lobby; ibid., 11–12.

13 The NYC Landmarks50 Alliance, created in late 2012, included the Historic Landmarks Preservation Center, Historic Districts Council, New York Preservation Archive Project, Landmark West!, New York Landmarks Conservancy, Municipal Art Society, and other preservationists, who were brought together by Diamonstein-Spielvogel to enhance public awareness of, and attention to, the 50th Anniversary. To develop greater public interest and involvement in the anniversary, it was thought to be essential to involve organizations and individuals from other fields—business, visual arts, film, music, dance, science, literature, finance—to participate in the commemoration. Approximately 190 organizations were involved. Projects included symposia; concerts; lectures; races; walking tours; exhibits; ringing the Nasdaq bell; flying an airplane banner around New York City; lighting the Empire State Building; commissioning a WNET video on preservation; gathering at the Four Seasons with Mayor

include historic preservation. The city is still recovering from the impact of the pandemic, with its rapid changes in societal norms and populations, disturbing empty storefronts, unused and seasonal restaurant sheds, and darkened office buildings. By the spring of 2023, the NYC Landmarks60 Alliance was organized to address the need for a comprehensive remembrance facilitated by collaborative endeavor; to raise public awareness and generate public involvement, each Alliance member agreed to create their own event, large or small. Throughout 2025, numerous events organized by the NYC Landmarks60 Alliance, and its members, friends, and associates will take place throughout New York City.

Committed to the enduring importance of New York City's landmark principles, we hope to create a lasting commemoration that involves contemporary and future thinking, inspires diverse viewpoints, and fosters widespread discussion and activities relating to historic preservation. Because of my long-standing interest in the significant art of the essay as a concise literary form, when I sought a more permanent expression of contemporary points of view, the idea for this publication took shape. The fortuitous convergence of these

---

David N. Dinkins; playing an artist's video on the Times Square Jumbotron and in elevators, taxicabs, and health clubs throughout New York City; panels of speakers; billboards with images of landmarks and the Alliance's axiom ("Honor Our Past, Imagine Our Future"); bus shelter posters; and the publication of a new, sixth edition of the comprehensive publication *Landmarks of New York*, which includes an updated history of the issues surrounding preservation as well as descriptions and photographs of designated structures and historic districts. The NYC Landmarks50 logo was designed by Massimo Vignelli as an homage to earlier streetscape projects; the logo was then "adaptively reused" for the 55th Anniversary by one of the NYC Landmarks50 Alliance members, Susan Demmet of the Murray Hill Neighborhood Association, and again for the 60th Anniversary with the addition of an image of a sparkler and the inclusion of the "Honor Our Past, Imagine Our Future" axiom.

Walter Leland Cronkite Jr.

November 4, 1916 – July 17, 2009

519 East 84th Street, Manhattan

Widely referred to as 'the most trusted man in America', journalist and CBS news anchor Walter Cronkite lived here from 1957 to 1999. Born in Missouri, Cronkite left the University of Texas in his junior year to work at The Houston Press. He then joined KCMO, in Kansas City, MO, as their news and sports radio reporter, where he met his future wife, Mary Elizabeth Maxwell. In 1937, he joined the United Press, for whom he covered WWII, from the Atlantic convoys through the Nuremberg Trials. Recruited by CBS News in 1950, he became news anchor and managing editor of the Evening News in 1962. For almost twenty years, his professional and fatherly persona calmly informed a sometimes turbulent nation. After his retirement in 1981, he continued as a special correspondent for CBS, CNN, and NPR until 2008, and wrote a syndicated column. The recipient of numerous honors, including four Peabody Awards for excellence in journalism, and the Presidential Medal of Freedom, he was known for his sign-off line "And that's the way it is..." He often quoted Thomas Jefferson, "A nation that expects to be ignorant and free, expects what never was, and never will be."

Historic Landmarks Preservation Center

two interests led to the commemoration of the 6oth Anniversary of the New York City Landmarks Law through this collection of essays.[14] My hope is that *Beyond Architecture: The New New York* will provide a lasting and energizing contribution to the 6oth Anniversary, while reflecting the world in which we live and telling a new New York story in many of its dimensions.

To reveal that story, a number of the most informed, knowledgeable, and imaginative thought leaders, seminal thinkers, scholars, critics, essayists, engineers, historians, architects, and landscape architects in New York City were invited to write freely on any and all of these issues and aspects of the built environment, including the role of historic preservation in a changing city, in order to present a wide range of viewpoints that we hope will encourage thought, action, and activism. It has been a genuine pleasure to work with these exceptional collaborators on this publication; profound thanks to Vishaan Chakrabarti, Justin Davidson, Andrew Dolkart, Thomas Dyja, Paul Goldberger, Adam Gopnik, Michael Kimmelman, Guy Nordenson, Nat Oppenheimer, A.O. Scott, Lisa Switkin, and Rosemary Vietor, a remarkable assemblage of gifted writers, thinkers, scholars, and visionaries committed to the public good, who helped us understand and envision New York City in novel and challenging ways.[15]

---

14 Since 1990, the PEN/America Diamonstein-Spielvogel Award for the Art of the Essay has annually honored an outstanding essayist whose corpus of work reinforces their enduring contribution to the art of the essay.

15 This "story" is about a New York City that, while devoted to tradition, is also endlessly changing. As noted by Dana Rubinstein and Emma G. Fitzsimmons, "New York City is nothing if not constantly in flux. Bodegas become illegal smoke shops. Neighborhoods identified with one group of immigrants become home to another. Disney supplants pornography in Times Square. Working-class outposts become havens for 20-somethings with trust funds"; see "It's Tough to Get Things Done in New York. Here's Why," *The New York Times*, June 14, 2024, https://nytimes.com/2024/06/14/nyregion/congestion-pricing-failure-nyc.html (accessed June 14, 2024).

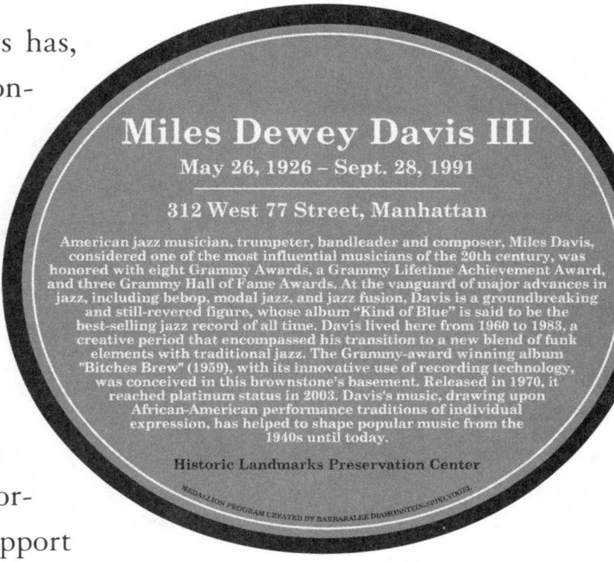

Each of these remarkable writers has, in this collaborative adventure, demonstrably moved beyond architecture to examine some aspects of the past, present, or future of New York City, the most dynamic city on earth.[16] This noteworthy group was asked to consider the different, sometimes unforeseen, ways in which historic preservation has, will, and should shape the city: its neighborhoods, communities, and various support systems, including housing, education, food, and traffic. The resulting collection of thoughts and insights on the impact, legacy, and current and future evolution of New York City examines, appraises, and evaluates the development, continuing vitality, and exhilarating spirit of the city. While you, the reader, may not agree with all of these views, I hope these distinctive voices and creative and careful analyses of a subject that, in sixty years (as far as I am aware), has not often been examined so thoroughly, and with such intellectual rigor, will stimulate thought, discussion, and action as we move toward a new New York.

A caveat: this volume contains a preponderance of male voices. In part, that imbalance reflects the current disparate status of women in the field of architecture. The Bureau of Labor Statistics reports that, in 2023, 31 percent of the 203,000 people working as "Architects, except Naval" in the United States were women.[17] However, those numbers may signify even more when we learn that 53 percent of students (both undergraduate and graduate) enrolled

---

16 With a population of more than 8.3 million, New York City's land area is approximately 469 square miles and includes 300 square miles of land, roughly equivalent to Kansas City, Missouri (population 509,000), and slightly larger than Augusta, Georgia (202,000). See https://www.census.gov/quickfacts /fact/dashboard/newyorkcitynewyork/PST045219 (accessed August 8, 2024).

17 For more details, see U.S. Bureau of Labor Statistics, "Architects, except Landscape and Naval" percentages for 2023 and 2019, at https://www.bls.gov/cps/cpsaat11.htm and https://www.bls.gov /cps/cpsa2019.pdf (accessed March 7, 2023).

The following text appears within a commemorative plaque image:

Miles Dewey Davis III
May 26, 1926 – Sept. 28, 1991

312 West 77 Street, Manhattan

American jazz musician, trumpeter, bandleader and composer, Miles Davis, considered one of the most influential musicians of the 20th century, was honored with eight Grammy Awards, a Grammy Lifetime Achievement Award, and three Grammy Hall of Fame Awards. At the vanguard of major advances in jazz, including bebop, modal jazz, and jazz fusion, Davis is a groundbreaking and still-revered figure, whose album "Kind of Blue" is said to be the best-selling jazz record of all time. Davis lived here from 1960 to 1983, a creative period that encompassed his transition to a new blend of funk elements with traditional jazz. The Grammy-award winning album "Bitches Brew" (1959), with its innovative use of recording technology, was conceived in this brownstone's basement. Released in 1970, it reached platinum status in 2003. Davis's music, drawing upon African-American performance traditions of individual expression, has helped to shape popular music from the 1940s until today.

Historic Landmarks Preservation Center

MEDALLION PROGRAM CREATED BY BARBARALEE DIAMONSTEIN-SPIELVOGEL

Ieoh Ming (I.M.) Pei

April 26, 1917 – May 16, 2019

11 Sutton Place, Manhattan

Ieoh Ming Pei, born in Guangzhou, China to Lian Jun Zhuang and Tsuyee Pei (a key figure in the creation of China's modern banking system), came to the U.S. to attend MIT, where he received his B.Arch (1940), and met Wellesley student Eileen Loo; they married in 1942. He received an M.Arch (1946) from Harvard. Two years later, developer William Zeckendorf, Sr. invited him to lead his new in-house architectural design team; early projects included Kips Bay Plaza in NYC (1957-62). By 1960, I.M. Pei & Associates was an independent firm. His selection to design the John F. Kennedy Presidential Library was followed by other prestigious commissions, including government and office buildings, hotels, museums, and a concert hall. His works include the National Gallery, East Building, Washington, DC (1968-78); Bank of China Tower, Hong Kong (1982-89); the Grand Louvre, Paris (1983-93), and the Museum of Islamic Art, Doha, Qatar (2003-08). Pei, the consummate architect/diplomat, received the 1979 AIA Gold Medal, the 1983 Pritzker Prize in Architecture, and the 1992 U.S. Presidential Medal of Freedom. The family lived here for almost 50 years, until his death in 2019.

Historic Landmarks Preservation Center

MEDALLION PROGRAM CREATED BY BARBARALEE DIAMONSTEIN-SPIELVOGEL

in accredited architecture programs from 2020 to 2021 were female. The disparity between those two numbers is important and suggestive.[18]

We invited eight remarkable women from the fields of architecture, design, conservation, and the law to participate, and four initially accepted. Unfortunately, the demands of life, their tight schedules, and professional calendars intervened, and only two were able to participate. We genuinely regret this limited representation, and hope that this volume will remind more architectural firms to provide additional opportunities for leadership and responsibility in every forum to the capable women they employ, and to support the expression of their viewpoints on these issues.[19] Inclusive representation of all participants in the complex mosaic of New York City—whether immigrants, minorities, women, or people with disabilities—is essential for our pluralistic society to function effectively, in accordance with our core values. With these acknowledged lacunae, we offer here a complex, but not comprehensive evaluation of the impact, legacy, current status, and envisioned future of New York City and its Landmarks Law—its effectiveness, its gaps, its achievements, and its potential.

As part of this commemoration, an ongoing goal of the NYC Landmarks60 Alliance is to assist in the development of new audiences and to nurture future preservationists, dedicated to enhancing their own and other communities through the preservation of their multiple histories. New York

---

18 *National Architecture Accrediting Board Annual Report*, 2022, 10, https://www.naab.org/wp-content /uploads/2022_NAAB_Annual_Report_final-1.pdf (accessed March 7, 2024).

19 See also Kendall A. Nicholson, "Where Are the Women? Measuring Progress on Gender in Architecture," Association of Collegiate Schools of Architecture website, June 2020, https:// www.acsa-arch.org/resource/where-are-the-women-measuring-progress-on-gender-in-architec ture-2/ (accessed March 7, 2023).

City has long been a gateway for immigration to the United States. In 2022, the foreign-born U.S. population was estimated at 46.2 million, more than half of whom lived in just four states, including New York. And in 2023, the Office of the New York State Comptroller observed that more than one in three New Yorkers (36.7 percent) were foreign-born. During the last sixty years, New York City has benefited from several major diasporas, notably Asian (in 2023, estimated to represent 14.5 percent of the population, or 1.2 million,[20] including Asian Indian, Korean, Bangladeshi, and Filipino), and Hispanic. As of 2024, immigrants from the Dominican Republic, Mexico, and Venezuela, and internal migrants from Puerto Rico, represent the majority of Spanish speakers in New York City, which, even by the 1990s, had already occasionally been described as a "minority majority" city.[21] Immigration, we believe, continues to be crucial to the continuing vibrancy of our country and our city.

We have reflected on how new New Yorkers could find a sense of belonging in a strange city; how long-held traditions are balanced with internal desires and external pressures for assimilation to a new environment.

---

20 According to the U.S. Census report of April 9, 2024, the other three states with large immigrant populations are California, Texas, and Florida; see https://www.yahoo.com/news/more-half-foreign-born-people-194238773.html?guccounter=1 (accessed April 10, 2024). See also U.S. Census Data, https://www.census.gov/quickfacts/fact/table/newyorkcitynewyork/RHI425222#RHI425222 (accessed April 3, 2024); and "Stability & Change in NYC Neighborhoods 2010 to 2020," NYC ARCIS Maps, https://storymaps.arcgis.com/stories/c7bf9175168f4a2aa25980cf31992342 (accessed March 11, 2024). Also see Winnie Hu and Jeffrey Singer, "Chinese Join Influx from Southern Border to New York," *The New York Times*, March 10, 2024, MB7, on the increased number of Chinese immigrants in New York, which notes that there were 52,700 Chinese immigrants to the United States during Fiscal Year 2023, twice the number for Fiscal Year 2021.

21 See Edward B. Fiske, "Minorities a Majority in New York," *The New York Times*, March 22, 1991, B1.

Bella Abzug

July 24, 1920 – March 31, 1998

2 Fifth Avenue, Manhattan

Born in The Bronx to Russian immigrants, Bella Abzug was a graduate of Hunter College (1942) and Columbia Law School (1947). A labor and civil rights lawyer, much of her work was pro bono defense for victims of injustice. A cofounder of Women Strike for Peace (1961), the national women's peace movement, and the National Women's Political Caucus (1971), created to increase women's participation in politics, she entered politics with a successful run for Congress (1970). On her first day there, Abzug introduced a bill to end the Vietnam War; in 1975, she introduced the first Congressional gay rights bill. After an unsuccessful bid for the U.S. Senate (1976), she left the House in 1977. Though she never again held elected office, Abzug remained dedicated to social action and politics, and co-founded the Women's Environmental Development Organization (1991). Married to lawyer Martin Abzug from 1944 until his death in 1986, they raised two daughters, Eve and Liz.

Historic Landmarks Preservation Center

MEDALLION PROGRAM CREATED BY BARBARALEE DIAMONSTEIN-SPIELVOGEL

As new New Yorkers seek to find reflections of their lives and their varied heritages—usually absent—in our city's historic built and commemorative environment, a further concern is how such absences have affected and will continue to affect their views on heritage and preservation, and, in turn, shape our city's future.

The vitality of a street, a neighborhood, and a historic district hinges on broader involvement by its residents. Many "discoveries" of previously hidden histories—for example, Weeksville's historic free Black community, detected in 1968; the excavation of the African Burial Ground, begun in 1991; and the discovery of an Underground Railroad station at the Parsons Nursery in Flushing, Queens, in 2016[22]—have often been cases of uncovering history hidden in plain sight, the results of efforts by small but significant organizations and citizen advocates. During the last fifty years, a similar desire for representation through publicly funded memorials has begun to emerge; a few sculptures have marked the beginning, additions that remain within the realm of traditional and long-established categories of commemoration.[23] While newer arrivals may not yet have established clear histories, trajectories, and vectors of influence that remain to be represented, the broader question remains—whose history is considered significant enough to preserve? And in what form? By

---

22 See Charlotte Jackson, "From the Archives: A Ticket for the Underground Railroad," Bowne House website, about their first discovery of this connection: https://www.bownehouse.org/ticket-for-the-underground-railroad (accessed April 3, 2024).

23 One recent example is the Mellon Foundation's Monuments Project, launched in 2020, a multiyear commitment "aimed at transforming the nation's commemorative landscape to ensure our collective histories are more completely and accurately represented." To date, support has been provided for eighty projects. For more information, see https://www.mellon.org/article/the-monuments-project-initiative (accessed November 30, 2023).

what mechanism? And by whose choice, jurisdiction, or priorities?

What we choose to designate as a landmark is not purely academic. It is also part of an ongoing tension between valid fear of the forces of gentrification that frequently accompany the imprimatur of landmark designation and the belief that designations by the Landmarks Preservation Commission have insufficiently represented both communities of color and immigrant neighborhoods, whose occupants historically gravitate to locales where their countrymen reside. In December 2023, Sarah Carroll,[24] the chair of the New York City Landmarks Preservation Commission since 2018 and a lifelong preservationist, said that the commission would "focus on inclusion . . . as a touchstone for the agency, an affirmation of the Commission's long-standing commitment to equity, codified in the Landmark Preservation Commission's 2020 Equity Framework,[25] in which the agency outlined its approach to ensuring diversity and inclusion in its designations, enhancing transparency and accessibility in its regulatory work, and ensuring designated buildings meet the evolving needs of all New Yorkers, including

---

24 Chair Sarah Carroll started her career at the LPC in 1994; she has served in various capacities over the past thirty years, including as landmarks preservationist, deputy director of preservation, and director of preservation. Prior to her appointment as chair in 2018, she served as executive director, managing the agency's operations and working closely with the chair to develop policy and strategic planning agency-wide. As executive director, she oversaw the designation of more than four thousand buildings and sites in the city, the implementation of numerous transparency and efficiency measures (including new website features that provide information and access to the agency's work), and the development of a new internal permit tracking database that increased efficiency and staff accountability in the application process. While the process is now much more efficient for the applicant, some have argued that the "juice" of lively public discourse, which depends on the back and forth between the public and the commission, has been lost with some of these changes.

25 For more information regarding the Equity Framework, see https://www.nyc.gov/site/lpc/about /pr2021/lpc-launches-equity-framework.page (accessed December 14, 2023).

Lorraine
Vivian Hansberry
May 19, 1930 – January 12, 1965

112 Waverly Place, Manhattan

The first African American woman to write a play performed on Broadway, Lorraine Hansberry is best known for *A Raisin in the Sun* (1959), about a Chicago family living under racial segregation. The play's title is drawn from Langston Hughes' poem, *Harlem*, and some of its elements are taken from her parents' life—their purchase of a home in a racially restricted Chicago neighborhood eventually culminated in the 1940 Supreme Court decision that restrictive covenants could be legally contested. In 1950, Hansberry moved to NYC, where she attended the New School, wrote for Paul Robeson's Pan-Africanist newspaper, *Freedom*, and, in 1953, married producer Robert Nemiroff. Later involved with the nation's first lesbian rights organization, The Daughters of Bilitis, Hansberry bought this building in 1960, where she resided until her death. Hansberry inspired Nina Simone's 1969 song, *To Be Young, Gifted and Black*.

Historic Landmarks Preservation Center
Greenwich Village Society for Historic Preservation

MEDALLION PROGRAM CREATED BY BARBARALEE DIAMONSTEIN-SPIELVOGEL

housing and increased climate resiliency."[26] Questions remain: Will there be a focus on architectural and cultural landmarks as new New Yorkers strive to celebrate their heritage within the architectural strictures of landmark designation? How will the heritage of new New Yorkers be preserved, celebrated, or even restored, when visible elements of their presence are not yet reflected within the city's built environment? And by whom?[27]

While most New York City families still seek the vigor and stimulation of our city's varied cultural offerings, lively social scene, and new restaurants, it is increasingly difficult to find affordable ways to live in the new New York. Structural changes to the city have been accompanied by social and cultural shifts. Many well-established cultural institutions have limited options other than relying heavily on aging and sometimes foreign populations as their primary audiences and supporters, while striving to spark widespread interest from younger or more diverse groups. At the same time, intriguing and admired cultural magnets have developed in "other" boroughs and "happening" places—for example, National Sawdust in Williamsburg, Brooklyn Youth Chorus in Cobble Hill, the Perelman Performing Arts Center in Lower Manhattan, the National Jazz Museum in Harlem, the Hip Hop Museum

---

26 Sarah Carroll, email communication to the author, December 6, 2023.

27 On October 25, 2023, the ground-breaking took place for The People's Theater: Centro Cultural Inmigrante—a new destination in Inwood, Manhattan, that co-funder Lin-Manuel Miranda noted is "about community, offering a space where art, culture, and identity converge"; see Anna Rahmanan, "Lin-Manuel Miranda Is Backing a Massive New Performance Arts Center in NYC," *Time Out*, October 26, 2023. This new cultural center may possibly be key to the preservation of the day-to-day traditions of some new New Yorkers, whose language, music, dance, and performing arts will find a home. How this new center will align itself with traditional ideas of neighborhood, community, preservation, and "entertainment" has yet to be parsed out, but is suggestive of a rich and complex future.

in the South Bronx, the new Louis Armstrong Center in Queens, and the still-nascent Centro Cultural Inmigrante in Inwood—organizations that seek to engage New Yorkers who pursue less traditional and less formal cultural activities that more accurately reflect their interests and traditions.

Amid this complexity, after sixty years, preservation continues to shape a rapidly changing and intricate cityscape. Ironically, we now see developers, who in the past might have resisted landmark designation, trumpeting the idea that their newly constructed building is a landmark—the designation a seemingly new status symbol.[28] While historic preservation has a noteworthy and often positive impact on quality-of-life issues for some New Yorkers, the conversations concerning preservation have changed. The diminishing availability of low-cost housing; expanding high-priced development; residential and commercial parking issues; the temporary postponement of congestion pricing; potential new giant garbage disposal containers;[29] outdoor dining; the increase in immigration

---

28 In a statement about his new building, Sir Norman Foster said, "425 Park Avenue will set new standards for workplace design and provide an *enduring landmark* [my emphasis] that is both of its time and timeless." Apparently the architectural team for 425 Park Avenue was so committed to this idea that they incised an inscription on the building: "Sir Norman Foster—A Landmark Building." For more information, see *The Architects Newspaper*, https://www.archpaper.com/2021/09/425-park-avenue-telescopes-skyward-with-diagrid-glass/ (accessed April 2, 2024); and Clifford A. Pearson, "A Full Block Office Building Rises on Park Avenue," *Architectural Record*, March 1, 2024, https://www.architecturalrecord.com/articles/16756-a-full-block-office-building-rises-on-park-avenue-for-the-first-time-in-half-a-century (accessed April 3, 2024). Tiffany & Co. now self-styles its renovated 57th Street and Fifth Avenue building as "The Landmark"; Andrew Russuth, "At Tiffany's Flagship, Luxe Art Helps Sell the Jewels," *The New York Times*, March 29, 2024, C1. Employees answering telephone calls verbally refer to the store as "the Landmark."

29 See Emily Badger and Larry Buchanan, "New York's Trash Is Two Journalists' Treasure," *The New York Times*, March 30, 2024, A2, https://www.nytimes.com/2024/03/30/insider/new-yorks-trash-is-two-journalists-treasure.html (accessed April 1, 2024).

Jonas Salk

October 28, 1914 – June 23, 1995

853 Elsmere Place, The Bronx

A graduate of Townsend Harris H.S. and City College (1934), Jonas Salk lived here with his parents and two younger brothers until the age of nineteen. He received an M.D. degree from New York University (1939), followed by a residency at Mount Sinai Hospital. Salk began his research career at the University of Michigan (1942), working on the first influenza vaccine. In 1955, he developed the first polio vaccine with his research team at the University of Pittsburgh, at a time when polio epidemics crippled tens of thousands in the U.S. annually. After the vaccine's success, he founded the Salk Institute for Biological Studies in La Jolla, California, where scientists research the causes, prevention and cure of disease. He was awarded a Presidential Citation from President Eisenhower (1955), a Congressional Gold Medal (1955), the Albert Lasker Award (1956), the Jawaharlal Nehru Award for International Understanding (1975) and the Presidential Medal of Freedom from President Carter (1977).

Historic Landmarks Preservation Center

and resulting competition for social services; continuing gentrification; climate change; and our shrinking coastline due to depleted groundwater systems and rising seas—these are all critical issues for New Yorkers.[30]

With 8.33 million estimated residents in 2024, New York City is the largest city by population in the United States—a city so large that it ranks higher in population than each of thirty-nine states.[31] While some few New Yorkers say they are ready to move on, others think New York is "still the best metropolitan city in the U.S.," with "the most convenient public transportation system in the country," and "culture and an ethnic diversity that makes it the most cosmopolitan city in America," as a long-term New Yorker recently observed in *The New York Times*.[32]

One key element is the ongoing evolution of community identity and involvement. Rather than accepting earlier, broad cultural norms, residents have a growing awareness of self-identity through their more specific and local cultural heritage and history. The accepted values of the mid-twentieth century have evolved to a more nuanced understanding that there are other voices to

30 The New York City poverty rate increased from 18 percent in 2021 to 23 percent in 2024; it was estimated that 50 percent of New York City families could not meet their basic needs and faced a housing shortage exacerbated by a rental vacancy rate of 1.4 percent; see Emma Fitzsimmons and Jeffrey Mays, "Has the City Bounced Back? For Some, But Not for All," *The New York Times*, March 10, 2024, MB7. Underscoring the rise of income inequality, New York City has been identified as having the fastest-growing millionaire and centi-millionaire populations in the world, and is a close second in growth in billionaires to the Bay Area; see https://www.henleyglobal.com/publications/wealthiest -cities (accessed March 28, 2024).

31 Winnie Hu and Stephanos Chen, "New York City's Population Shrinks by 78,000, According to Census Data," *The New York Times*, March 14, 2024. See Britannica, "List of U.S. States by Population as of 2023," at https://www.britannica.com/topic/largest-U-S-state-by-population; and U.S. Census Quick Facts, at https://web.archive.org/web/20210426202412/https://www2.census.gov /programs-surveys/decennial/2020/data/apportionment/population-change-data-table.pdf (accessed April 2, 2024).

32 Dan Nelken, quoted in "Reader Corner from the Comments Forum," *The New York Times*, March 28, 2024, A3.

hear, and that it is important that they be heard. And while much of the activism of this stance, especially during the pandemic, took place through social media, attention must be paid to the many neighborhood block associations and local organizations that continue to foster a sense of community in New York City. During the last sixty years, these often modest grassroots organizations have been the crucible of activism in countless arenas—greening streets, improving roadway safety, securing tenants' rights, reducing street crime, fighting for better schools, and, yes, preserving their distinctive neighborhood character, quality, and history.[33]

As new values come into play, the preservation and enhancement of the built environment—New York City's architectural heritage and history—remains a priority, though the reasons for its importance have shifted over the past decades. In the early years of this work, preservationists were occasionally viewed as irrationally tied to the past, but the scientific and economic reasons for supporting historic preservation have begun to emerge into the public discourse on urbanism during the last few decades.[34] By

---

33 When discussing the key role of New York City citizens in making change, the exemplary and unparalleled work of citizen-activist Bette Midler must be acknowledged. In 1995, she founded the nonprofit New York Restoration Project, which has partnered with government, community groups, and individuals to plant thousands of trees, preserve and renovate community gardens, restore parks, and transform open public space throughout New York City's five boroughs; see https://www.nyrp.org/en/ for more information.

34 We use the term "urbanism" with some reservation. Since two boroughs—Brooklyn and Queens—are comparable to or greater in population than major cities such as Chicago, Houston, or San Diego, the New York City megalopolis elicits questions of a different order: whether New York City is no longer a city, but a linked series of large urban areas, and how that might affect best practices in governance. For a brief exploration of the megalopolis, see James Cheshire and Michael Batty, "The Era of the Megalopolis: How the World's Cities Are Merging," *The Conversation* website, November 22, 2022, https://theconversation.com/the-era-of-the-megalopolis-how-the-worlds-cities-are-merging-193424 (accessed March 28, 2024).

Jackson Heights, Queens, has been called "the most culturally diverse neighborhood in New York, if not on the planet," according to *The New York Times*, July 21, 2024. The Scrabble Sign is inspired by the work of local Queens resident Alfred Mosher Butts, the architect who invented Scrabble in the basement of Community United Methodist Church, located on the block where the sign was installed. At its 2011 installation are (left to right) Assemblymember Francisco Moya, Historic Landmarks Preservation Center Chair Barbaralee Diamonstein-Spielvogel, Councilmember Daniel Dromm, and State Senator Jose Peralta. PHOTO: COURTESY OF THE *QUEENS GAZETTE*.

encouraging adaptive reuse, the protection of historic buildings can lead to a more educated use of existing resources. As builders realize that once-cheap materials, such as cement and concrete, are nonrenewable and increasingly expensive, adaptive reuse and preservation of existing structures is starting to be more generally perceived as both climate-friendly and economical.

Moving beyond the utility of preservation, we should acknowledge its sociological function and psychological impact. The preservation of familiar neighborhood landmarks and historic buildings builds greater commitment to neighborhoods, as personal landmarks remain, even when transformed by new uses. Many writers have observed that each of us carries our own New York within us, something, perhaps, that neighborhood preservation organizations have always known. Whether native New Yorker, longtime transplant, or recent arrival, we each have our own set of "landmarks" that tells us where we are and where we might be going. As the now-classic *Learning from Las Vegas* suggested more than fifty years ago, every New Yorker is, to some degree, in thrall to the power and the symbolism of architectural form. Landmarks—whether buildings that we, as a society, have deemed important enough to designate, or simply structures that have become familiar to us—are part of our internal cognitive maps. And when we share elements of those cognitive maps with others, we create social cohesion.

Landmark buildings and landmark spaces offer us perspective, a sense of identity, and memories. They shape our experience and, most of all, provide us with an awareness that some things last longer than mortal existence. With this growing understanding of the powerful rationales behind historic preservation, it is our hope that, rather than devolving into a routine

Barbaralee Diamonstein-Spielvogel with Mayors Abraham Beame, David N. Dinkins, Edward I. Koch, and Rudolph Giuliani. PHOTO: JOAN JEDELL.

"Trivia Moments" in the MTA (Metropolitan Transit Authority), a contest created through a partnership between NYC Landmarks60 Alliance and OUTFRONT Media, challenges commuters to prove their knowledge of New York City and compete every week to win free subway and bus rides. Public engagement as of August 2024 included 38,826 website visits and 21,215 QR code scans to access the information and contest. PHOTOS: OUTFRONT MEDIA.

#65

What classic novel, set in Brooklyn, focuses on the life of a young girl and her immigrant family?

governmental review, a box to be checked before development and construction, the preservation of our historic built environment will be acknowledged for its manifold values and contributions.

The significant architectural heritage to which we are committed is supported by the many alternative histories that constitute our city. Diversity has been and remains our strength. Though sometimes hidden, these alternative histories are integral, though still unknown, parts of a more familiar story that may emerge over time. Although most new New Yorkers have yet to have their histories woven into the physical fabric of our architectural heritage, the new New York, in all its complexity, should be embraced as a significant part of our future. This slender volume, *Beyond Architecture: The New New York*, discusses a range of these critical issues and plausible concerns as we seek to craft a forward-looking vision of New York City that honors our past, celebrates the present, and imagines a resilient future. ᪥

Only two trees have been designated landmarks: the Weeping Beech Tree in Flushing, Queens, designated in 1966, and the *Magnolia grandiflora*, shown here, designated in 1977. The Weeping Beech was brought as a cutting to the United States by Samuel Bowne Parsons in 1846, and is no longer extant. The *Magnolia grandiflora*, a rare species for this northern climate, was grown from a seedling in the mid-1880s by William Lemken and planted in front of his house in Bedford-Stuyvesant, Brooklyn. PHOTO: BENJAMIN SWETT.

George Stacy (photographer), *The Bowne House*, circa 1860, albumen stereograph. The back of the photograph is inscribed "Old Daddy Bowne's House, Flushing, L.I." PHOTO: LIBRARY OF CONGRESS.

ROSEMARY VIETOR

ONE HOUSE, ONE FAMILY, THREE CENTURIES OF NEW YORK HISTORY

DESIGNATED AS A NEW YORK CITY LANDMARK on February 15, 1966, and named to the National Register of Historic Places in 1977, the Bowne House, the oldest house in Queens, holds an importance that "lies not only in its age and charm but also [in] its association with religious freedom in America." The house has been owned and operated as a museum by the Bowne House Historical Society since 1947; its preservation can be attributed to the care of seven generations of the same family, from its construction circa 1661 up until its current incarnation as a house museum. Rather than adapting the structure to changing times and needs, "each succeeding generation sought to adapt themselves to the revered house."[1] The Bownes and their descendants were, perhaps, the first preservationists in New York City.[2]

As a member of the family, I grew up with many stories of the old house and, as with my forebears, family history had a major influence on my life. In 1935, in his address celebrating fifty years as a minister, my great-grandfather, the Reverend R.F. Norton, noted, "My ancestry was prevailingly Quaker"—possibly the foundation of his interest in religion and public

---

1   See Gordon William Fulton, "The Bowne House, Flushing, New York: A Historic Structure Report," Graduate School of Architecture, Planning, and Preservation, Columbia University, 1981. See also Richard Wheeler Walter, "The Bowne House—Flushing, Queens County, New York: An Historic Structure Report" (Albany, NY: Hartgen Archaeological Associates, Inc., 2006).
2   For more information about the Bowne and Parsons family histories, see Herbert Parsons, "History and Genealogy of the Parsons and Bowne Families, Including an Account by James Parsons, 1791, of the Parsons and Yates Families," manuscript, New York, 1881.

service—commenting that he "sometimes . . . sat for a few moments in the pew which Trinity Church has given to our family in perpetuity because one of our ancestors had given $70,000 to that church, the interest to be used for the daily distribution of bread to the poor." Although he died before I was born, I was fortunate to have spent many days with the eldest of his eight children, my grandmother. Her only grandchild, I looked forward eagerly to my visits. Her cupola-topped house was filled to the attic with family memorabilia and childhood treasures: stained glass, portraits, photographs, books, an old piano. Those varied items and her memorable family stories became, in turn, the basis for my interest in my family's past.

As an adult, I was reintroduced to the Bowne House as a member of its board of trustees. The story of the preservation of the house and its collections is compelling. So many other historic properties have passed out of the hands of their original owners and have been demolished or inappropriately readapted. New York City has few remaining seventeenth-century buildings, and little is left of the original village of Flushing, called Vlissingen by the Dutch, once an agricultural area closely tied to the history of Long Island. Flushing remained relatively bucolic until 1939, when it became the site of the World's Fair and its urbanization began.

While the Bowne House itself is an interesting historical structure, as many have noted, it remains of such great interest after more than three centuries primarily because of the events that took place there early in its history—events that altered the course of American history.

That story begins here.

JOHN BOWNE

On June 11, 1661, "We went from our haus at fflushing towards rodiland [Rhode Island] to the generall meeting [of the Quakers] where we did stay nyne days time, and the twentie eaight day of the same month about the midel of the day we came home agennne." This entry in John Bowne's journal, now preserved at the New-York Historical Society, is his first reference to the Bowne House and helps date its construction, while also showing his

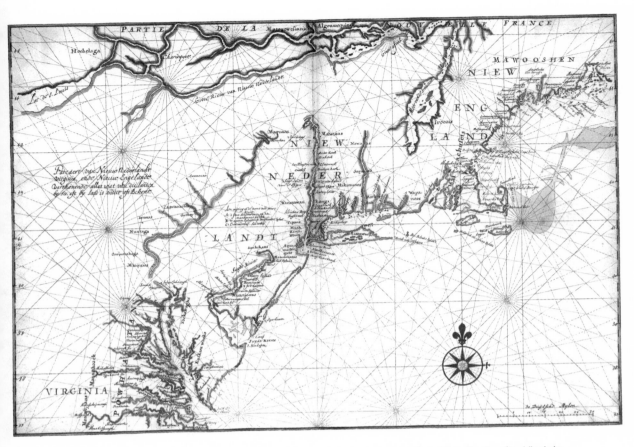

Joan Vinckeboons, *Map of the Northeast Coast of the United States from New England to Virginia* (detail), 1639, pen-and-ink and watercolor. The map shows the English and Dutch colonies along the coast during the period when twenty-two-year-old John Bowne emigrated from England in 1649 with his father and sister to become colonists. After a brief residence in the Boston area (Niew England), his family moved to Flushing (Vlissingen), part of New Netherland (Niew Nederlandt), where he met and married Hannah Feake, a Quaker.
PHOTO: LIBRARY OF CONGRESS, THE ATLANTIC WORLD: AMERICA AND THE NETHERLANDS.

involvement with the Quaker community. The house and its neighbor, the Flushing Quaker Meeting House, less than half a mile distant, are two surviving seventeenth-century buildings from this community of English settlers.

John Bowne had left his home in Matlock, Derbyshire, England, in 1649 with his father, Thomas, a widower, and his sister Dorothy, traveling first to the Massachusetts Bay Colony. No record has been found regarding the reason for their departure, but England was in turmoil from the violent Civil War. King Charles I had been arrested, imprisoned, and, in January of that year, executed.

The Bownes had lived in the Matlock-Bakewell area for centuries. They owned extensive properties there, and the family farmed and operated lead mines. Lead was a valuable commodity and a source of wealth. Today the area is known as the Peak District, designated as an "Area of Outstanding Natural Beauty" for its parks and scenic vistas. John had been born in 1627 and baptized that year in St. Giles' Church, Matlock (Church of England). He returned to England a number of times during his life, once for a copy of his baptismal record at St. Giles. From the Massachusetts Bay Colony, in 1651, the Bownes moved south to Flushing. John Bowne married Hannah Feake, and they started their family, eventually having eight children.

The first of the momentous events that led to the preservation of the Bowne House took place only one year after the construction of the house, as Bowne writes in his journal: "In the yere 1662 nustile [New Style] on the first day of the 7th month [September] Resolved [Waldron] the scout [Sheriff] came to my house at vlishing [Vlissingen/Flushing] with a company of meen with sords and gonns." Waldron was there under the orders of Peter Stuyvesant, the Dutch governor of New Amsterdam and an ardent Calvinist.

The events that brought Waldron to the Bowne House began, in part, with the 1657 Flushing Remonstrance, which later became codified as the First Amendment of the U.S. Constitution, guaranteeing an individual's right to freedom of worship as part of the Bill of Rights. The year before, in 1656, Director-General Peter Stuyvesant had passed an ordinance that anyone who provided housing for a Quaker meeting for a single night would be fined, and that any vessel bringing a Quaker into the province would be confiscated.[3]

In response to this ban, and in accord with the Flushing Charter of 1645, which granted to all "to have and Enjoy the Liberty of Conscience, according to the Custome and manner of *Holland*,"[4] it was decided by the

---

3 See "Three Centuries of Activism," https://www.bownehouse.org/three-centuries-of-activism (accessed March 20, 2024).

4 "Charter, Granted by the Director and Council of New Netherland to the Town of Flushing," October 10, 1645, from N.Y. Deed Book, II. 178, in *Laws and Ordinances of New Netherland, 1638–1674*, edited by E. B. O'Callaghan (Albany, 1868); for the full text of the charter, signed by Willem Kieft, see https://static1.squarespace.com/static/5e29d4d91e118a3f8cb62233/t/5eca85eob6e 5372e0ef99961/1590330848533/Kieft+Charter+of+Flushing+text.pdf (accessed March 20, 2024).

Flushing residents, in 1657, to send a remonstrance to Stuyvesant in protest of his action. The origins of both the Flushing Charter and the Flushing Remonstrance can be traced back nearly one hundred years, to the 1579 treaty called the Union of Utrecht.[5] That document avowed the right to "freedom of conscience," a concept that underlies the later language of the Remonstrance. While both repression and tolerance were exercised in Holland and its colonies, the written laws of the Union of Utrecht created the framework for the expectations of Flushing residents—so clearly expressed in both the Flushing Charter and the later Flushing Remonstrance—that they and any visitors to the Dutch settlement, part of New Netherland, would be able to "remain free in his [*sic*] religion and that no one shall be investigated or persecuted because of his [*sic*] religion." As one historian has noted, one of the most significant exports of the Dutch was the concept of tolerance—"one of the keys to the success of the Dutch Golden Age."[6] The passionate response of settlers to Governor Stuyvesant's ban is more easily understood, given this broader context.

This eloquent Remonstrance for religious freedom—originally written in Dutch, authored by Tobias Feake,[7] and written down by clerk Edward Hart[8]—was signed by thirty local Flushing residents,[9] none of them

5   The Union of Utrecht, signed on January 23, 1579, was an agreement between the provinces of Holland, Zeeland, Utrecht, Gelderland, Friesland, and the rural districts of Groningen. Article XIII of the Union states: "As for the matter of religion, the States of Holland and Zeeland shall act according to their own pleasure, and the other Provinces of this Union shall follow the rules set down in the religious peace drafted by Archduke Matthias, governor and captain-general of these countries, with the advice of the Council of State and the States General . . . and no other Province shall be permitted to interfere or make difficulties, provided that *each person shall remain free in his religion and that no one shall be investigated or persecuted because of his religion*, as is provided in the Pacification of Ghent" (my emphasis).

6   See Russell Shorto, "The Importance of Flushing," *New York Archives* (Winter 2008): 8–11.

7   It has been suggested that Tobias Feake was Hannah Feake Bowne's cousin; see https://www.wikitree.com/wiki/Feake-6.

8   See "The Flushing Remonstrance Revisited," New York State Archives Partnership Trust, https://www.nysarchivestrust.org/exhibits/flushing-remonstrance (accessed March 20, 2024).

9   Although John Bowne was not a signatory, his brother-in-law, Edward Farrington, was one of the signers of the Flushing Remonstrance. For a full list of signatories, see "The Flushing Remonstrance, 1657," https://history.nycourts.gov/about_period/flushing-remonstrance/ (accessed March 21, 2024).

Quakers,[10] who nevertheless requested an exemption to Governor Stuyvesant's ban on Quaker worship. The final paragraph of the Remonstrance reads:

> The law of love, peace and liberty in the states extending to Jews,[11] Turks and Egyptians, as they are considered sonnes of Adam. . . . Therefore if any of these said persons come in love unto us, we cannot in conscience lay violent hands upon them, but give them free egresse and regresse unto our Town, and houses, as God shall persuade our consciences, for we are bounde by the law of God and man to doe good unto all men and evil to noe man. And this is according to the patent and charter of our Towne, given unto us in the name of the States General, which we are not willing to infringe, and violate, but shall houlde to our patent and shall remaine, your humble subjects, the inhabitants of Vlishing.[12]

The prescient words of this petition were ignored by Governor Stuyvesant, who punished both Feake and Hart and continued to enforce his ban on religious diversity.

By permitting and welcoming a group of Quakers to gather in his home for worship, John Bowne openly defied Stuyvesant's edict that no one was to worship anywhere other than in the Dutch Reformed Church. When discovered, Bowne was arrested by the sheriff, transported by boat to Manhattan, sentenced to pay a fine, and, upon his refusal to pay, imprisoned for several months.[13] Stuyvesant, determined to be rid of him, banished him from the colony and had him transported to England in late 1662. Bowne was forced to leave behind his wife, several children, and his elderly father, Thomas.

---

10 Kenneth T. Jackson, "A Colony with a Conscience," *The New York Times*, December 27, 2007, https://www.nytimes.com/2007/12/27/opinion/27jackson.html (accessed March 20, 2024).

11 In contrast to the tolerance of the Dutch, which earned Amsterdam the sobriquet the "Jerusalem of the West," we should remember that other nations confined Jews to ghettos, restricting their movement and their livelihoods. The earliest ghetto was established by decree in Venice in 1516; see "The Jews in Venice (1516–1797)," https://www.ghettovenezia.com/en/the-history/; and "The Jews in Holland," from *The Voice of Israel*, ed. R. H. Herschell (London, 1845), vols. 1–2, 27.

12 For the full text of the Flushing Remonstrance, see https://history.nycourts.gov/about_period /flushing-remonstrance/ (accessed March 14, 2024).

13 Bowne writes of his trial and imprisonment, "Journal of John Bowne, Folio 51," reproduced at https://www.bownehouse.org/three-centuries-of-activism (accessed March 20, 2024).

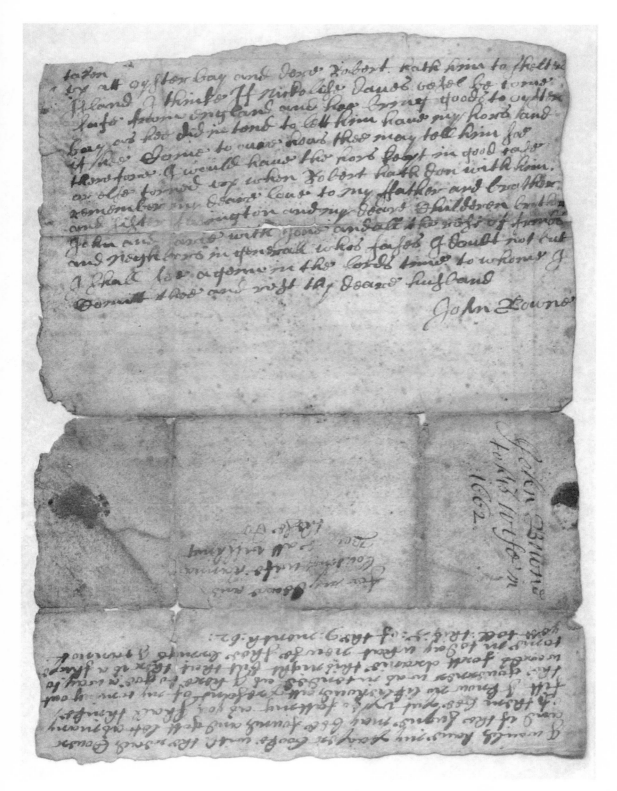

Letter from John Bowne to Hannah Feake Bowne, his first wife and the mother of his eight children. The letter was sent in 1662, when he was incarcerated in New Amsterdam for the offense of holding forbidden Quaker meetings in the colony of New Netherland.

He arrived in England in January 1663 and made his way to Holland to plead his case before the Dutch West India Company. He carried with him a copy of the 1645 Flushing Charter,[14] which guaranteed members of the Flushing community "liberty of conscience in the manner and custom of Holland." Bowne, who did not speak Dutch, brought with him a translator from England and used his Quaker connections in Ireland, England, and Holland to help him appeal his case.[15] His plea before the company utilized the language of the charter when he challenged the edict of Governor Peter Stuyvesant against the practice of religions other than the Dutch Reformed Church. Bowne's nonviolent protest against Stuyvesant's edict was the first to succeed.

The trial of John Bowne before the Dutch West India Company was the first successful legal test of religious freedom in America, a principle enshrined more than one hundred years later in the First Amendment of the U.S. Constitution. Because of this trial, the rights of assembly and freedom of speech were also guaranteed—principles advanced by John Bowne in 1662, when he welcomed Quakers into his house.

In 1664, John Bowne returned triumphant to his family in Flushing and, in 1669, made the first of a series of alterations and additions to what had been a modest one-room farmhouse. The Bowne family had prospered; John continued to farm and also sold books and other necessities as the family became one of the more affluent in the town. In the tradition of his English homeland,[16] he continued to add to his landholdings, becoming one of the largest landholders in Flushing; he acquired several hundred acres there, as well as land in New Jersey and Pennsylvania.

Today, the Bowne House occupies a tiny fragment of what had been several

---

14 "Charter, Granted by the Director and Council of New Netherland to the Town of Flushing" (see note 4).

15 See Arthur Worrall, "Journal of John Bowne 1650–1694" (review), *Quaker History*, Friends Historical Association 65, no. 2 (Autumn 1976), https://muse.jhu.edu/article/393790/pdf (accessed March 20, 2024).

16 For a detailed exploration of English Land Law in the seventeenth century, see Charles J. Reid, Jr., "The Seventeenth-Century Revolution in the English Land Law," *Cleveland State Law Review* 43, no. 2 (1995): 221–302, https://engagedscholarship.csuohio.edu/cgi/viewcontent.cgi?article=1607&context=clevstlrev.

hundred acres of family property, located in what is now bustling downtown Flushing. However, it holds a larger place in our history, and it is due to this

> associative value in American history that the house of John Bowne, as a tangible artifact of his existence, has been venerated these past three centuries. It is only recently that its intrinsic architectural value has been recognized, but without the association it had with John Bowne and religious freedom, it would have long since disappeared, like almost every other example of building in the 17th century in this area.[17]

Bowne died in 1695 and is buried in the churchyard of the Old Quaker Meeting House (now a National Historic Landmark).

Despite his meticulous record keeping, John Bowne left no will. Ownership of the house at his death passed to his and Hannah's surviving son, Samuel, who continued to occupy the house with his wife, Mary Becket, and their children. Samuel and his family remained until his death in 1745, when he left the house to his son John in a deed of gift dated 1740.

His son John then left the property to his second son, also a John. The will stipulated that his son John was to receive the house on his twenty-first birthday (1764). Although Samuel's widow continued to occupy a section of the house, John's will stated that "the house and farm where I now reside, have been for nearly a century and a half the residence and property of my Ancestors" and he wished it to remain "to my descendants." Later generations of the family continued John Bowne's tradition of preservation of the house and interest in civic engagement; many were committed Quakers. Notable descendants included Robert Bowne.

ROBERT BOWNE

Robert (1744–1818) was the child of Samuel's son John; he left Bowne House to establish Bowne and Company in 1775. Located in downtown Manhattan, in the South Street Seaport area, Bowne & Co. prospered, but in the shadow

---

17 See Fulton, "The Bowne House Flushing, New York" (note 1).

of uncertainty. In 1776, many New York City shops had closed. The Declaration of Independence had been signed in Philadelphia, and the gilded statue of King George III had been pulled down from its pedestal in Bowling Green by an angry mob. As a Quaker, Robert was not enthusiastic about the Revolution, and he and his family fled Manhattan.

When the Revolution ended in 1783, Bowne & Co. reopened to sell stationery supplies and to begin printing work.[18] By this time, the business was sufficiently successful that Robert was able to turn his attention to philanthropic interests, one of which was the abolition of slavery. In 1785, the Manumission Society was founded. George Clinton, Alexander Hamilton, John Jay, Robert Bowne, Thomas Eddy, and others were named directors. Their founding resolution stated:

> The Society, viewing with commiseration the poor African slave, will exert all lawful means to ameliorate his sufferings and ultimately to free him from bondage and to impart to him the benefits of as much education as seems best calculated to fit him for the employment and right understanding of his future privileges and duties when he shall become a free man and citizen.

The Society's goal was to end the practice of enslavement in America. Quakers had begun to discourage the ownership of slaves among their members by the mid-eighteenth century; by 1770, they had banned the practice altogether among their members, so that Quakers who did continue to own slaves were excommunicated.

In addition to the cause of manumission, Robert Bowne was also involved in the establishment of Free Schools. The private and church schools that existed in New York City were not adequate to address the urgent needs of a growing immigrant population. In order to teach children the language

---

18 Dean Failey, *The Bowne Family and Patterns of Patronage—Study for the Bowne House* (New York: The Bowne House Historical Society, Museum Advisory Committee, 2006).

of their new country, its history, and basic skills, a group was formed to discuss the problem. The Society for Establishing a Free School in the City of New York included De Witt Clinton, John Pintard, Archibald Gracie, Colonel Henry Rutgers, John Murray Jr., and Robert Bowne. Pupils were to be chosen on the basis of need, irrespective of "sect, creed, nationality or name." This effort was the beginning of the New York City public school system.

Other civic-minded endeavors by Robert Bowne included his service as governor at New York Hospital for thirty-four years; his work as first chair of the New York Health Committee, which was formed to address the yellow fever epidemic of 1793; and his position as one of the first twelve directors of New York's first bank—the Bank of New York—whose board included Alexander Hamilton, John Vanderbilt, and Isaac Roosevelt. He was also involved with the Mutual Insurance Company, formed to provide fire insurance in downtown Manhattan, and was an early proponent of the Erie Canal. Robert Bowne had organized an "inland Navigation Company" in 1791 to explore options, but due to his death in 1818, he did not see the canal open in 1825. Nevertheless, his contributions were recognized by Governor De Witt Clinton, who, in April 1824, refers to Robert Bowne's work as a canal commissioner:

> Let me on this occasion discharge a debt of gratitude and of justice to the late Robert Bowne. He had at an early period devoted his attention to this subject and was master of all its important hearings. To his wise counsels, intelligent views and patriotic exercises, we are under incalculable obligations.[19]

The Erie Canal energized the economy of both New York City and New York State, bringing prosperity and enabling the state to earn its imperial nickname.

---

19 Robert Bowne *Minturn, Memoir of Robert Bowne Minturn* (printed for private circulation; New York: Anson D. F. Randolph & Co.), 16.

THE PARSONS FAMILY

In the nineteenth century, the Bowne House passed to Mary Bowne Parsons and her husband, Samuel Parsons. Born in New York in 1774, Samuel Parsons is described as studious and "remarkable for the sympathy and benevolence with which his heart seemed imbued . . . devoted to the relief of suffering." In 1806, after what was described as a happy childhood, "he married Mary, daughter of John and Anne Bowne of Flushing, where he purchased a farm, originally part of the Bowne homestead."[20]

There, in 1838, Samuel established, with his sons, Robert and Samuel Jr., the famous Parsons Nursery.[21] From the mid-seventeenth century, Flushing flourished as an area of tree culture and horticulture. The Flushing nurseries were well known; William Prince had established his nursery there in 1737. The plants cultivated in the area were considered so desirable that both Presidents George Washington and Thomas Jefferson visited in search of fine specimens. The Prince nursery was sufficiently important that General Howe placed troops there to guard it during the Revolution.

In addition to being the home of several nurseries, Flushing was rumored to be a hotbed of abolition activity, a safe haven for the Underground Railroad, with a number of "safe houses"—and one of these reported locations was the Bowne House. The Underground Railroad refers to the network of escape routes and hiding places used by freedom seekers before the American Civil War. Escapees usually fled to Northern states where slavery had been abolished and often continued north to Canada. As a Quaker community,

---

20 See Parsons, "History and Genealogy of the Parsons and Bowne Families" (note 2).

21 Samuel Parsons is also known for planting the remarkable Weeping Beech tree that lived from 1847 to 1998 in Flushing, Queens. It was one of the few trees in New York City to be designated an individual landmark (designated in 1966, prior to the creation of the scenic landmark category). While traveling through Europe, the Flushing nurseryman purchased the seedling in Belgium and later planted it on the grounds of his nursery near the Bowne House. According to the New York City Department of Parks and Recreation, in the tree's maturity, its branches touched the ground and re-rooted, creating a ring of offspring surrounding its immense canopy, which reached 60 feet in height and 80 feet in diameter. See https://www.nycgovparks.org/parks/margaret-i-carman -green, https://s-media.nyc.gov/agencies/lpc/lp/0142.pdf (accessed March 14, 2024); and Barbaralee Diamonstein-Spielvogel, *Landmarks of New York*, 6th ed. (New York: New York University Press, 2016), 172.

Mary Bowne Parsons (1784–1839) inherited the Bowne House with her mother and sisters following the death of her father, John Bowne III. In 1806, Mary married Samuel Parsons, a Quaker minister and famed nurseryman. None of Mary's sisters married, and ownership of the Bowne House passed to the Bowne/Parsons family. PHOTO: THE BOWNE HOUSE HISTORICAL SOCIETY.

Flushing had a history as a refuge for blacks both free and enslaved. The multicultural nature of the community had begun with its inception. As noted earlier, the 1657 Flushing Remonstrance had petitioned Governor Peter Stuyvesant for tolerance and acceptance of not only Quakers but also "Jews, Turks and Egyptians." In continuance of the Bowne family's commitment to the preservation of individual freedom and social responsibility, both Samuel and Mary Parsons were ardent abolitionists, as was their son Robert.

Samuel traveled the world in search of rare and unusual plant material;

his property eventually included several hundred acres in and around downtown Flushing, with additional agricultural land in Florida. The nursery had a flourishing business in the Southern states, and the Flushing location, with its dense plantings and proliferation of outbuildings, likely provided excellent cover for the family's recently confirmed Underground Railroad activities.

Flushing was an important way station owing to its position on the water and because of the antislavery sentiments of the community. According to the census records, William Bowne Parsons, aged twenty-seven, lived at Bowne House with his elderly aunts and unmarried siblings. His occupation is given as "horticulturalist," like his older brothers Samuel and Robert Bowne Parsons, who ran the Parsons Nursery. The nursery and surrounding wooded areas would have been good areas for freedom seekers to hide; there is no evidence to date that they were concealed in the house itself.

Underground Railroad activities had to be clandestine. Not only were freedom seekers themselves at risk of exposure and punishment, but also those who aided and housed them were subject to significant fines. The Fugitive Slave Act of 1850 stipulated that freedom seekers be returned to their owners, even from a free state. Those found to be assisting a freedom seeker could be subject to a substantial fine or imprisonment. Few records of these activities survive; concealment was critical to the success of the operation. Remarkably, the Bowne House has located in our archival collections, and in materials from other sources, confirmation of the family's Underground Railroad involvement.

In 2022, based in part on the discovery of these materials related to the Underground Railroad, the Bowne House was recognized for the strength of its archival holdings by the United States National Park Service. The house has been designated a member of their National Underground Railroad Network to Freedom program, and a facility for the research of the Underground Railroad and abolitionist activities in New York State. Bowne House is the only site in Queens to be so designated.[22]

---

22 Charlotte Jackson, "A Ticket for the Underground Railroad," Bowne House website, notes how this evidence came to light: https://www.bownehouse.org/ticket-for-the-underground-railroad (accessed April 10, 2024).

The last family members to occupy Bowne House, the Parsons sisters Bertha and Anna, left in the mid-1940s. They were then in their nineties, and, mindful of the history of the Bowne House, they had preserved the house and its contents while making as few changes as necessary, including updating plumbing and electricity. The Parsons sisters did admit a few guests for occasional tours. They enjoyed wearing Quaker dress, and neighborhood accounts recall the sisters sitting on the porch of the house to watch local children pass by on their way to school.

When the last sister left to go to an assisted-living facility, a group of local citizens formed to purchase the property. Enthusiasm for the project was such that hundreds of people, even schoolchildren, supported it. The house, with some of its furnishings, was acquired by a group of local residents with an eye toward opening it as a museum. Mayor Fiorello La Guardia chose to give an address on October 10, 1945, in the same room where John Bowne had been arrested, when the mayor dedicated the house as a museum on the three-hundredth anniversary of the signing of the Flushing Town Charter—the document that John Bowne had carried with him during his banishment, imprisonment, and trial almost three hundred years earlier to secure "freedom of conscience in the manner and custom of Holland" for the original settlers of Flushing. The house opened to the public in 1947.

There is no doubt that the strong commitment of generations of Bowne and Parsons family members to honor their ancestors, and preserve and maintain the house, its contents, and its legacy for future generations, ensured the survival of the Bowne House. For three hundred years, the legacy of this simple dwelling has been entwined with the family's passionate commitment to individual freedom and their powerful sense of social responsibility—principles that inspired them to preserve their modest home as a reminder of significant moments in our national history. As we continue to uncover the complex history of Flushing and the Bowne family, one is thankful for those early instincts of preservation that have permitted us to continue to explore this rich and exciting story. 🏛

The façade of Grand Central Terminal (1913) includes the sculpture Glory of Commerce, with representations of Minerva (wisdom), Hercules (strength), and Mercury (speed and transportation). Designed by Reed & Stem and Warren & Wetmore, the terminal occupies 48 acres and has forty-four platforms, more than any other railroad station in the world. PHOTO: ZACK DEZON.

PAUL GOLDBERGER

THE STATE OF PLAY:
LANDMARKS AT SIXTY

THE PASSAGE OF LEGISLATION in 1965 to formally empower the New
York City Landmarks Preservation Commission was an act of boldness tem-
pered by timidity. The legislation set out what would be the most ambitious
program of historic preservation that any major city in the United States had
ever attempted. Until the New York City Landmarks Preservation Commission was created, preservation of buildings by legal order had been tried only
in smaller cities or in specific sections of larger cities, such as in the French
Quarter in New Orleans, where the creation of the Vieux Carré Commission
in 1936 was the first instance in the United States in which a public entity was
given the legal power to preserve privately owned historic buildings. New
York's Landmarks Preservation Commission came nearly three decades later,
and it had jurisdiction over not just a single historic neighborhood but the
entire breadth of the largest city in the United States.

However, the law New York passed in 1965 was not quite as intrepid
as it seemed. New York, after all, has always been a city defined largely by
the values of commerce, particularly by the values of real estate, and the real
estate industry saw the Landmarks Law mainly as a threat to its hegemony:
to save any old building, however worthy, was to deny the opportunity to
build a new one. As the particulars of the law were debated in the city council, several council members who shared the real estate industry's belief that

building, not preserving, was the DNA of New York demanded that the powers accorded to the Landmarks Preservation Commission in the original draft of the legislation be reduced. The final version of the law gave the commission only eighteen months to designate official landmarks; after that period, the commission's work would go on hiatus for three years, during which it would, for all practical purposes, have no power at all.

After the three-year moratorium, the law specified another designation period of only six months, followed by another hiatus of three years, a pattern that would repeat indefinitely, thus assuring that the commission would stay on the sidelines most of the time. Developers, of course, operated under no such limits, and the moratorium gave the real estate industry six times as much time to demolish and develop new buildings as the commission had to protect old ones. The city council also required that buildings not be eligible for consideration until they were thirty years old, and it removed other provisions in the early drafts of the law that would have allowed the commission to designate architecturally significant public interiors and that would also have given it authority over buildings adjacent to designated landmarks in an attempt to acknowledge the importance of context.

The Landmarks Law was a compromise, like so much legislation in New York and everywhere else, and it would hardly bring New York City into the promised land of preservation. It is common to think of the law as having been passed in response to the outcry over the demolition of Pennsylvania Station in 1963, but in fact the station was only the most traumatic of many losses in the 1950s and 1960s that led New Yorkers to question whether they could trust that the city's best works of architecture were safe from sudden disappearance. And the losses hardly ended with the demolition of Pennsylvania Station, which was followed closely by the demolition of the Savoy-Plaza, McKim, Mead & White's sumptuous hotel designed as a companion to the Plaza Hotel, which went down as the Landmarks Law was making its way through the legislative process, and the demolition of the Brokaw Mansion at Fifth Avenue and 79th Street, a massive stone château that was torn down in February 1965, quite intentionally demolished just under the wire

Park Avenue between East 68th and 69th Streets, showing Pyne-Davison Row, a group of four neo-Georgian townhouses built between 1909 and 1926, saved from demolition by the intervention of the Marquesa de Cuevas, the former Margaret Rockefeller Strong, granddaughter of John D. Rockefeller Sr. PHOTO: MUSEUM OF THE CITY OF NEW YORK.

to avoid any possibility that the pending legislation might in some way tie the hands of the developers who wanted to replace the enormous house with a high-rise apartment tower.

The loss of the Brokaw Mansion followed perhaps the only positive news of the time, which was that one of the city's greatest intact assemblages of townhouses—which filled the west side of Park Avenue between 68th and 69th Streets and included two houses by McKim, Mead & White, one by

Delano & Aldrich, and one by Walker & Gillette—was saved at the last minute by an anonymous purchaser, who snatched the properties away from a developer who had already begun to demolish the interiors as he prepared to erect a high-rise apartment building. The rescuer turned out to be the Marquesa de Cuevas, a Rockefeller cousin who chose to extend her family's philanthropic reach into historic preservation. But the nature of this last-minute preservation drama only underscored the urgent need for a more reliable legal mechanism for preservation: after all, the city could hardly count on rich private patrons to step in every time. And dozens of other important buildings were in danger.

Once the Landmarks Preservation Commission was finally given legal authority, its limits were made clear by its inability to act when, in the immediate aftermath of the adoption of the city's landmarks legislation, the Singer Building, Ernest Flagg's magnificent tower of 1908, briefly the tallest building in the world, fell to make way for a much larger but far less distinguished office tower. And the Landmarks Commission would be powerless to designate the old Metropolitan Opera House, largely because its most distinguished element was its auditorium, and the commission could not designate interiors as landmarks. Because city parks also could not be designated, neither could the commission have a say in how the Metropolitan Museum of Art extended its footprint more deeply into Central Park when it planned its major expansion during the commission's early years.

Still, for all its shortcomings, the law would nevertheless have a profound effect, not just on the shape of New York City but on the national preservation movement. In what was a tacit admission by the city that the first attempt at giving historic preservation the force of law had not brought about the disaster for the city that the real estate industry had predicted and had in fact been popular, eight years after Mayor Robert Wagner signed the original legislation, John Lindsay, the next mayor, signed an amended Landmarks Law that eliminated the moratorium periods. The new law allowed the commission to designate landmarks on a continuous basis and added new categories of designations for interior landmarks and for public parks as scenic landmarks. The Real Estate Board of New York offered a tepid protest, claiming that the revised law would stifle development, but the revised law passed by a vote of 36 to 0, as clear a sign as there could be that by 1973, if not by 1965, the preservation of important buildings had become an expected part of the political and cultural landscape of New York.

While opponents of the Landmarks Law had succeeded in eliminating the category of interior landmarks from the original 1965 legislation, they did not remove the category of historic districts, which confers a degree of protection on dozens of buildings in a single swoop, similar to that for individual landmarks. In effect, historic district designation is designating landmarks on a wholesale rather than a retail basis, and over time it has proven to be one of the most potent tools in the preservation arsenal. Brooklyn Heights and the western portions of Greenwich Village were the city's first historic districts; over the six decades of the Landmarks Preservation Commission's existence, historic district designation has gone beyond these upscale neighborhoods to encompass a remarkably diverse array of neighborhoods, from Mott Haven in the Bronx to Crown Heights in Brooklyn and Addisleigh Park in Queens.

As of March 2024, more than 37,900 buildings in New York City were under the protection of the New York City Landmarks Preservation Commission, the vast majority of which are in 157 historic districts and are not individually designated landmarks. These numbers seem large, yet all the historic districts combined represent only 2 percent of the land in the city, and the total number of protected buildings is less than 4 percent of the one million buildings in New York City. The city itself is emphatically not a historic district. In fact, in the last generation, the volume of new construction, particularly high-rise construction, has soared, and it is not hard to think of New York in the twenty-first century not as a city that preserves its past, but as a city that builds as eagerly, and sometimes as aggressively, as it has throughout its history.

Still, sixty years after the passage of the original legislation, and fifty-two years after the amended Landmarks Law gave the commission more of the tools the original drafters of the law had envisioned for it, no one is challenging the city's right to protect its architectural heritage, including those parts of it that are privately owned. We are nevertheless long past the time when New York City was, in one critical instance, the most important advocate for historic preservation in the United States, when its attorneys successfully argued before the Supreme Court their right to preserve Grand Central Terminal for the benefit of the public. When the court decided in favor of the city in 1978, upholding not only the designation of Grand Central but the constitutionality of the Landmarks Law, it was a defining moment for historic preservation—the first time that the Supreme Court had given constitutional backing for the notion that historic preservation could be seen as a public good, and therefore a justifiable exercise of the government's authority. The Penn Central Railroad's plan to erect a skyscraper atop Grand Central, effectively disfiguring the landmark, was dead, and the city's other great railroad station would never suffer the fate of Pennsylvania Station.

For all that the preservation movement was a popular cause with widespread citizen support, it would not have been brought into being without the help and guidance of a number of the city's more patrician political and business leaders. These New Yorkers included Geoffrey Platt, who became the first chair of the Landmarks Preservation Commission; Albert Sprague Bard, Whitney North Seymour, James Grote Van Derpool, Otis Pratt Pearsall, and Harmon Goldstone, among others, who played major roles in getting the legislation passed, ran the commission in its early years, and managed the Grand Central case. They were conservative, traditional men of power who surely thought of themselves as more elite than the real estate developers they were often opposing. But it was a time when conservatism and commitment to the public welfare did not seem mutually exclusive, when the city's business and political leaders, however much they may have been largely white, male, and Anglo-Saxon, tended to believe that they had an obligation to improve the city and not just to make money. They believed in the notion of the public realm, both as a physical entity and as a conceptual one, and the idea of a citizen's responsibility to contribute to the common good. The period leading up to the passage of the original landmarks legislation in 1965 and extending through the Grand Central decision in 1978 appears to have been one of the rare times in New York's history in which a portion of the city's gentry and many of its committed citizens worked in tandem toward a common goal. It was, in some ways, one of the last gasps of the twentieth century's period of High WASP statesmanship, played out on a local level.

This is but one of the reasons that the Supreme Court decision on the Grand Central case seems, in retrospect, to have been the triumphant moment in the history of the New York City Landmarks Preservation Commission. The commission had fought all the way to the Supreme Court to save one of the nation's great buildings; the decision, written in an opinion by Justice William Brennan Jr., seemed to underscore the preeminence of New York as a city and its importance as a leader in the national historic preservation movement. It did more than ensure the preservation of one of the city's greatest works of architecture. The Court also agreed with the city's assertion that saving landmarks was in the public interest and thus affirmed the right of the government to preserve privately owned buildings as a public good, in effect establishing the constitutionality of the landmark designation process. The ambitions of the city's many preservationists, whose labors so often seemed futile beside the power of the real estate industry, now appeared to be realized.

With the Grand Central decision, thirteen years after the passage of the New York City Landmarks Law, the nation's highest court had made it clear that the city, and thus any governmental jurisdiction, could determine the fate of certain buildings so long as their owners were provided with some potential compensation, which, in the case of Grand Central, was the potential to sell the development rights to nearby properties. Before the 1965 landmarks legislation, the only check on the power of the real estate industry other than the economic forces of the marketplace was the city's ability to regulate development through zoning laws. Now, the right of the city to declare individual buildings as landmarks as well as entire neighborhoods as historic districts was a key additional tool to regulate development that had been validated by a decision by the Supreme Court.

If the 1978 Grand Central decision represented the culmination of what might be called the grassroots origins of the historic preservation movement in the United States, driven by citizens upset at the pace of change as well as at the quality of so much new architecture, it was never solely a populist effort, particularly in New York, where—to say it one more time—the support of what might be called an enlightened portion of the city's professional establishment was key to the movement's early success. After 1978, however, preservation would often be less of a grassroots effort. Private organizations, such as the venerable Municipal Art Society of New York (started in 1893 by a group of enlightened residents eager to promote better architecture in that era), led the citizens' effort to support the city government's pro-preservation stance in the Grand Central case, boosted by the impassioned backing of Jacqueline Kennedy Onassis and by the pro bono assistance of several of the city's most eminent law firms. Victory in the Supreme Court would make the Municipal Art Society larger, more established, and in many ways more conservative, as the real estate industry, aware that preservation was now a permanent force in New York City, began to see the benefits of cooperating with the society and with other allied groups, such as the New York Landmarks Conservancy, a private organization founded in 1973 that provides financial and advisory support to the owners of landmarked properties.

A new preservation establishment had arisen. It consisted not only of organizations like the Municipal Art Society and the Landmarks Conservancy, but also of many members of the real estate bar, who realized that preservation law was increasingly becoming an area of legal practice in itself, and of wealthy donors to preservation causes, who were recognizing that historic preservation was not merely a matter of saving a handful of quaint buildings, but a force that had the potential to have a major impact on the future of the city. On its surface, this growth was good news, but it would come, over time, to have a price as the preservation movement, no

The Villard Houses, 451–457 Madison Avenue, Manhattan, Historic American Buildings Survey, after 1933. These six Italian Renaissance–inspired mansions, built around a central courtyard by architects McKim, Mead & White (1882–1884), were commissioned by Henry Villard, a railroad magnate, newspaper publisher, philanthropist, and one of the most prominent financiers in the nation. PHOTO: LIBRARY OF CONGRESS.

longer powerless, became accustomed to playing a role in the political and social maneuvering that shaped the city—and thus, like every other player in the drama of city politics, saw the value, not to mention the necessity, of compromise.

Still, those years were not without substantial victories. As the Grand Central case worked its way through the legal system, preservationists won a significant battle over the Villard Houses, an extraordinary group of McKim, Mead & White brownstone mansions on Madison Avenue that had been designated a landmark in 1968, but whose integrity was threatened by the builder Harry Helmsley's plan to slice off the eastern portion of the houses and erect a skyscraper hotel. The Landmarks Preservation Commission, along with the Municipal Art Society, succeeded in preserving most of the threatened portion of the structure, requiring Helmsley to save its important interior spaces and integrate them into the hotel and to lease one wing of the historic structure to a consortium of civic groups that would locate their offices, shared meeting spaces, an exhibition gallery, and an architecture bookstore within it. The facility, called the Urban Center, would remain for thirty years as a perfect exemplar of adaptive reuse: a gathering place for people interested in the betterment of New York's physical environment in one of its most revered landmarks.

Other triumphant moments would occur for the Landmarks Preservation Commission, including its rejection in 1981 of a commercial skyscraper proposed by St. Bartholomew's Church to rise behind its Bertram Goodhue–designed Byzantine edifice on Park Avenue. The church sued the commission, asserting virtue by arguing that it would use the income from the office tower to serve the poor, but the commission prevailed. There would not be many instances after St. Bart's, however, in which the Landmarks Preservation Commission would argue as definitively, and as successfully, that a large and highly conspicuous real estate project would damage the city's cultural heritage and thus be contrary to the public interest.

More common was compromise, shown occasionally in a reluctance to support proposals to designate specific landmarks, but more often in a gradual willingness by either the commission or by citizens' preservation groups to accept many large-scale projects that might have offended preservationists and advocates of good design in the past. Not long after the St. Bartholomew's drama, for example, the Municipal Art Society's board was divided on the merits of opposing an enormous, twin-towered skyscraper planned for the site of the New York Coliseum at Columbus Circle. The society sued the city to block the project, then ultimately settled when the developer made a moderate reduction in size and replaced the original architect with a respected designer who happened to have been a member of the MAS board. Reprising the boldness and determination to fight the corporate power of the Grand Central case would prove, then, to be short-lived. In the end, the issue became moot as the stock market crash of 1987 derailed the Columbus Circle mega-project, at least temporarily. It came alive again late in the following decade and was ultimately built, at which point the MAS did not oppose it.

The Columbus Circle brouhaha was a reminder of the extent to which preservation and city planning, never unrelated, were becoming increasingly intertwined. The fight over the new Columbus Circle was not, strictly speaking, a preservation issue at all—the only notable building facing demolition was the banal Coliseum, whose protection had never been sought by even the most ardent historic preservationist. What was clear was that the Coliseum, a structure of moderate size, was to make way for something many times its height and bulk. The dispute brought into heightened focus what had become more and more obvious in recent decades: the new buildings rising in New York were, almost without exception, much larger than the older buildings they replaced, and many preservation efforts were driven less by admiration of what was there than by fear of what would replace it. An ordinary brownstone on a side street might not be a masterpiece, but to most preservation advocates its pleasant façade and welcoming scale were vastly preferable to any large apartment or office tower that might take its place. In the view of many of the city's advocates of good planning, design, and historic preservation, preventing bigger buildings was reason enough to campaign for preservation, and often, for landmark designation.

This argument was rarely, if ever, expressed directly. Using the city's authority to designate landmarks as a way of blocking new buildings that were felt to be undesirable was never the intention of the legislation, and it was not within the Landmarks Preservation Commission's purview to cite disapproval of a potential new building as a justification for designating an existing one. Still, preventing unwanted development had long been, for many citizens, a significant part of the appeal of historic preservation. It was, in effect, the unspoken rationale behind much of the public's participation in efforts to save landmarks and protect historic districts. As the city revised its zoning laws in the twenty-first century to allow more larger buildings in more sections of the city, including in some cases within historic districts, the commission seemed, to many citizens, all that stood between them and a city that consisted of nothing but shiny glass and steel skyscrapers.

The commission would disappoint them, at least much of the time. Cognizant of the absence of a legal mandate to function as a land-use agency, which was the province of the City Planning Commission, and mindful also of its uneasy position as a part, at least marginally, of the city's real estate establishment, the Landmarks Preservation Commission has seemed increasingly unwilling to take on major developers, prominent institutions, or even wealthy individual homeowners. In the years since the triumphant Grand Central decision, while the commission continued to designate actively, it tended to avoid the kind of direct confrontations with powerful interests that the Grand Central case, and later the St. Bartholomew's case, embodied. Not only, for example, did the commission not designate Huntington Hartford's Gallery of Modern Art at Columbus Circle—an idiosyncratic but iconic mid-century modern work by Edward Durell Stone—but also it declined even to hold a hearing on the merits of the building, deferring to the city administration, which wanted no obstacles in the way of its plan to sell the property to facilitate its reconstruction into a new museum.

Neither was the Union Carbide Building, one of Midtown's greatest postwar office towers, ever the subject of a hearing; the building, designed by Natalie de Blois of Skidmore, Owings & Merrill, was demolished by its owner, JPMorgan Chase, to make way for a new headquarters building by Foster + Partners, now under construction and due to be completed in 2026. If there was at least some compensation in the hope that this time one important building would be replaced by another—recalling the era, long ago, when buildings like the Lenox Library gave way to the Frick mansion, the Century Theatre was replaced by the Century Apartments, and the original Waldorf-Astoria Hotel was demolished to make way for the Empire State Building—that was not the case with other losses of the time, such as the Jacob Dangler House, a magnificent French Gothic mansion in the Bedford-Stuyvesant section of Brooklyn. A developer had already purchased the building and requested a demolition permit, a circumstance under which the commission was required by law to act within a limited time frame. This time the commission did hold a hearing, but its lack of a decision about designating the building during the statutory time limit led to the building's demolition.

The biggest problems the Landmarks Preservation Commission has faced in recent years have been those that, ironically, are a result of the extremely high property values in many historic districts. Not only did the loss of value that the real estate industry had predicted in 1965 not come to pass but, in many historic districts—such as Greenwich Village, Brooklyn Heights, the Upper East Side, and SoHo—property values became almost unimaginably high, squeezing out the diverse communities that had originally shaped these neighborhoods and making the properties susceptible to intense real estate speculation. Historic district status made high-rise development unlikely if not impossible, but that made the existing properties even more valuable to owners with deep pockets who could afford to turn existing buildings, which often had contained multiple apartment units, into vast private mansions.

Sometimes, damage to landmarks during the process of alteration made them, in the view of their owners, unsalvageable, a situation that may well have been the result of inadequate supervision by both the Landmarks Preservation Commission and the Department of Buildings. In recent years the commission has agreed to the demolition of several landmarked properties after approving renovations that posed significant dangers to their structures, including a row of six houses on lower Ninth Avenue in the Gansevoort Market Historic District and, most famously, the 1827 brick house at 14 Gay Street in Greenwich Village where the book and play *My Sister Eileen* and the musical *Wonderful Town* were set. The Gay Street house, along with several of its landmarked neighbors, was sold to a developer who, in the process of doing work that the commission had approved to convert the properties to elaborate luxury residences, severely damaged the foundation of No. 14. The commission agreed with the developer that the building was not salvageable.

This 85-story supertall mixed-use tower is planned to replace the Hyatt Grand Central New York hotel. With a projected 2.1 million square feet of office space, abutting and dwarfing the once-grand Grand Central Terminal, the new building is estimated to be completed in 2030. PHOTO: SOM/BOUNDARY.

Hyper-gentrification has created other preservation challenges as well. In the hope of increasing the city's stock of affordable housing, the de Blasio administration undercut historic preservation by increasing the permissible height and bulk in certain historic areas, such as SoHo, to allow larger development on vacant sites than had previously been permitted. However well-intentioned, the provision is unlikely to add significantly to the city's stock of affordable housing, given that the exceedingly high land prices in areas such as SoHo make a so-called affordable building implausible without a level of subsidy that federal, state, or city governments do not offer. The likelihood is that the up-zoning will bring not affordable housing but more luxury towers, compromising the architectural integrity of the historic district with no clear social benefit in exchange.

The development pressure the city faced during the first decades of the Landmarks Preservation Commission's existence, powerful as it seemed at the time, now appears almost modest. Preservationists were, for the most part, happy warriors, proud to be taking on the real estate industry in favor of a livable city and gratified to have a new and earnest city agency as their ally. It is a long time since the lines have been as neatly drawn as they were in those early years, and now, a quarter of the way through the twenty-first century, they seem more blurred than ever.

The Landmarks Preservation Commission is rarely at the table as far as major projects are concerned. In perhaps the most visible recent example, the commission had only an advisory role in the design of a proposed 83-story office tower to replace the Grand Hyatt Hotel to the east of Grand Central Terminal, symbolically the city's most important landmark. The vast building would not only overwhelm Grand Central to an extent that no other building does but also block the view of the Chrysler Building, the city's most beloved skyscraper crown, from the west and compromise it from elsewhere. And it could well make the 59-story Met Life (originally Pan Am) Building, once the largest commercial office building in the world and long disdained as an oversized intruder over Grand Central, look small for the first time in the sixty-two years of its existence.

The commission did not have the authority to block the project of its own accord. But it chose not to use its advisory role as a bully pulpit to take a stance on the serious issues that the new tower raises, such as the impact of new construction on adjacent landmarks, the notion of context, and whether buildings adjacent to Grand Central that use its air rights, as this building would, should be subject to landmarks review. It is a theoretical question, but a very real one: does the transfer of Grand Central's air rights to an adjacent site make that site, in effect, part of Grand Central and therefore under Landmarks Preservation Commission jurisdiction also? And then, of course, there is a more abstract question, which is what it means when the most famous part of a landmarked skyscraper is barely visible any longer: is the construction of a tower that blocks the view of the Chrysler Building tantamount to the destruction of this landmark by rendering its most important element invisible? After all, the commission has long used the standard of visibility from the street to determine whether certain alterations to landmarks are acceptable: if a rooftop addition cannot be seen from the street, for example, it is more likely that it will be approved. But what if a new building blocks the view of a landmark altogether? While the tower on the Grand Hyatt site has yet to be built, several new buildings of great height on or adjacent to Fifth Avenue in the 20s have already blocked the view of the Empire State Building from Madison Square and much of Fifth Avenue, robbing this neighborhood of what has long been its defining vista. The landmark has effectively disappeared.

Situations like this are, if nothing else, an ironic reminder that early drafts of the Landmarks Law had proposed giving the commission authority over buildings adjacent to landmarks. In the case of Grand Central and Chrysler, of course, the planned new building bridges the space between two of the greatest works of architecture ever built in New York and will affect them both significantly. But the Landmarks Law gives the commission no authority to deny the developers the right to move forward, or even to have any meaningful role in directing the design of the new tower. Views of landmarks, or view corridors toward them, are not protected. And given that the commission has said little in terms of public comment regarding either the planned neighbor of the Chrysler Building or the elimination of the view of the Empire State Building, it seems disinclined even to acknowledge this complex issue, let alone to address it directly. The fact that the same real estate industry that before the Landmarks Law was passed had predicted that the legislation would cripple its ability to function productively now, after sixty years of landmark designation, appears to have more power than ever only heightens the irony.

Now, in the third decade of the twenty-first century, the landmark designation process has come to be seen as just another of the many challenges and complexities to doing business in New York: not as a cultural good, but as one more bureaucratic hurdle to be crossed. The sense of mission that guided the founding generation of historic preservationists in New York is largely absent, replaced by a dutiful bureaucracy that rarely speaks with a strong voice and seems often to act as if it will support the protection of the city's architectural heritage best by keeping its head down, focusing on the minutiae of cosmetic alterations to buildings within historic districts rather than on larger issues that are likely to provoke major controversies.

The notion that historic preservation is a liability rather than an asset to the city's development has never gone away, although now it seems to be expressed by forces other than those of the real estate industry. In 1993, Herbert Muschamp, then the architecture critic of *The New York Times,* lamented of the architectural climate of New York that "the overarching problem was not change but the pervasive fear of change," and suggested that a culture that focused too much on retaining the past would be unwelcoming to new ideas. And if Muschamp, a passionate advocate of innovative new architecture, saw the historic preservation movement, and therefore the Landmarks Preservation Commission, as an obstacle to his hopes for the city, more recently Binyamin Appelbaum, an economist and member of the editorial board of *The Times,* pointed his finger in the same direction, although without even Muschamp's naïve earnestness about the ability of architecture to make urban life better. Appelbaum argued that the preservation movement was standing

One of the sixty-seven libraries constructed for New York City with the support of steel magnate Andrew Carnegie, the 1905 Classical Revival Tremont Library, designed by Carrère and Hastings, was designated a landmark by the New York City Landmarks Preservation Commission in March 2024. PHOTO: NEW YORK PUBLIC LIBRARY.

in the way of New York's ability to provide for its citizens. In an essay entitled "I Want a City, Not a Museum," Appelbaum suggested that the city was unduly fixated on preserving older buildings and that this was responsible for the lack of affordable housing in New York. "New York is not a great city because of its buildings," he wrote. "It is a great city because it provides people with the opportunity to build better lives."

Neither accusation makes much sense. At no time has the commission been hostile to new architecture, and in the years since Muschamp's essay New York has probably built more advanced architecture than it had in the decades preceding it. While the city's need for more affordable housing is acute, no evidence suggests that the problem could be solved by relaxing the provisions of the Landmarks Law. Indeed, Vishaan Chakrabarti of the architecture firm PAU studied the problem and reported that half a million housing units could be built in New York on sites that are empty and available if only the city would loosen some of its many non-landmark-related building restrictions and expedite construction. There is no need to make landmarks a whipping post. The perception of both critics is that the Landmarks Preservation Commission has too much power, which Muschamp felt it used to stifle creativity, and Appelbaum believed it used to stifle growth. There is no small irony in the fact that historic preservationists are more often heard to complain about the limited power of the commission and, more to the point, about its apparent reluctance to exercise many of the powers it does have.

The climate in New York now bears little resemblance to that of the early days of the Landmarks Preservation Commission, when it may have acted with hesitation but was gradually growing in courage, and the Grand Central case could be fought as if it were a moral crusade. Now, it is hard to know what an equivalent moral crusade would be, at least as far as historic preservation is concerned. The urgent issues in New York today—immigration, the availability of housing, the cost of housing, the city's infrastructure, and its transit system—are not problems that the commission could address even with the most laughably grandiose expansion of its powers. Yet neither are these problems ones that the commission created or has in any way exacerbated.

In the minds of some of the commission's critics, it has tried to stop time, to deny the inevitability of change; to others, the commission has allowed time to move too fast and has done too little to curtail the massive tsunami of development that has swept over New York in the past generation. In fact, some of the commission's better decisions in recent years have been those instances in which it has managed not to stop time but to slow it down and assert itself positively into the process of the city's evolution. One

Crowned by a colossal broken pediment that sets it dramatically apart from earlier Midtown glass skyscrapers, and often referred to as the Chippendale Building, this collaboration by Philip Johnson with John Burgee is considered by many the first postmodern skyscraper. PHOTO: ALEX FRADKIN/ THE OLAYAN GROUP.

of its most successful interventions in recent years was in 2018, when it stepped in to confer landmark designation on 550 Madison Avenue, the so-called Chippendale skyscraper by Philip Johnson with John Burgee, a gesture that stopped a new owner's plans for drastic and unsympathetic renovations of the building's celebrated postmodern façade. The plans were changed in 2019 to be much more respectful of the original architecture, and the commission enthusiastically supported the revised design. At the same time, however, it approved a plan for more radical changes to the rear of the building, over the objections of a few preservation fundamentalists but with the support of many others who cared about the building, including John Burgee, Johnson's former partner. The commission declined to consider the building's lobby a candidate for designation as an interior landmark, which troubled the most ardent preservationists but few others. The entire episode of 550 Madison Avenue was, in the end, a rare moment in which the commission was decisive, acted strongly and promptly, and demonstrated that preservation could, under the best circumstances, be both protective of the city's architectural heritage and helpful in reshaping a building toward new and different uses.

The problem is that there are too few stories like 550 Madison Avenue and too many like the one involving another significant work of postmodernism, 60 Wall Street by Kevin Roche, which has an unusual interior public atrium that is among the city's most notable postmodern interiors. Yet 60 Wall Street did not even rate a hearing before the commission when the building's owners announced their intention to demolish the atrium and redesign it as a conventional office building lobby. Interior public spaces are the purview of the City Planning Commission, the Landmarks Preservation Commission said, ignoring its own potential jurisdiction and seemingly abandoning the belief that architecture of the postmodern period had lasting value, as it had claimed to justify the designation of 550 Madison Avenue not long before.

The future of a city of mega-buildings will never turn on the fate of a single lobby, or even of a single building. That is not the point. Development and change will always shape a living city, and the New York landmarks legislation was crafted not to deny this, but to accept it and to use the tools of preservation to make the city more seasoned, more nuanced, more civilizing as an environment in which to live and work. The point is to embody the premise that, as Lewis Mumford so memorably put it, "In a city, time becomes visible."

New York will never be Paris and it will never be Venice or Amsterdam, but thanks to the Landmarks Law it has not become Hong Kong or Shanghai either, or, for that matter, Houston or Atlanta or Miami. After sixty years of official landmarks preservation, the city still struggles between its impulse to build and its impulse to preserve, its passion for the new in constant tension with its belief that things were better in times past, or at least that the buildings those times gave us were more appealing. The struggle will probably go on forever—the struggle itself, and the angst that surrounds it, are defining to New York's character.

What makes things different now is not the fact of change, but the scale at which building takes place. There are more and more buildings, and they are larger and larger than they have ever been. And it is not just the scale of the buildings themselves; it is also the vastness of the amounts of money at stake, as the city becomes, more and more, a place of private excess and public scarcity, a place in which the private sector, and particularly the financial services industry, makes decisions based on short-term gain, not on long-term social and civic benefit.

All of this has a cumulative effect on the city's psyche, and it certainly contributes to a sense of powerlessness that explains, at least in part, the absence today of a large public constituency zealously fighting preservation battles as there was in the early decades of the Landmarks Preservation Commission. The large civic groups are cautious, and apart from the Greenwich Village Society for Historic Preservation in lower Manhattan, Landmarks West on the Upper West Side, and the venerable Brooklyn Heights Association, there are few effective neighborhood-based local groups in historic districts. Early preservation victories were often won by advocates who could see landmarks battles as both a mission and a matter of nuanced, strategic politics. But now it sometimes seems as if the preservation community is divided between a tiny handful of preservation fundamentalists and the far larger economic and social forces pushing for mega-growth, with the commission in the middle, appearing ever more hapless.

Only a few years ago it would have been unthinkable that either the Empire State Building or the Chrysler Building—which more than any other towers have been the cherished symbols of the city's skyline—would be surpassed in height by newer skyscrapers not once but many times, and that both would be at risk of being rendered invisible by other towers crowding around them, as they are today. It is not surprising that people increasingly turn to the landmark designation process as a way of trying to deflect new construction; it may not be what the framers of the law intended, but it often feels like the only tool available to register dismay at the preponderance of enormous towers fueled by global investment capital. As the city grows bigger, the significance of preservation, sadly, seems only to get smaller.

The Empire State Building (1931) by Shreve, Lamb & Harmon, completed in only 410 days of construction, casts a shadow over Midtown Manhattan. Until its completion, the 1,046-foot Chrysler Building (1930) was the tallest building in the world due to the addition of a 185-foot spire. At 102 stories, the Empire State Building was the world's tallest building until the first tower of the World Trade Center topped out in 1970. PHOTO: CHRISTOPHER ANDERSON/MAGNUM PHOTOS

"TEAR DOWN AND BUILD OVER AGAIN"

NEW YORK FEELS EDGIER than it has in a long time. We're not talking *Taxi Driver* edgy—anyone who tells you that either wasn't around then or hasn't been back since. But some of that Every Man for Himself energy has definitely oozed into our lives again; we're dropping trash and running yellows. Trying to get home before the streets get too dark. We're alive but we're restless and no Sondheim revival, rap beef, or new donut store can distract us from the feeling that we're all out here just floating right now, waiting for something to happen. To those who rode the doom loop to Miami and other sunny, tax-free ports we say farewell. The world's greatest brains, brawn, and beauty still come here; so do huddled masses yearning to breathe free. They come here to find out what's next. But right now we seem to have no clue. While we've been talking about recovery, New York has outgrown its skin, the way it does every few decades.

As Walt Whitman wrote, it's time to "Tear Down and Build Over Again."

Of course, Whitman himself wasn't entirely in favor of it. Back in 1845, when he published "Tear Down and Build Over Again" in the *American Review*, there were no promises if you were a building. Eternity was for the Pyramids. New York in 1845 was change and speed—the telegraph had just been invented; trains were new. It must have been a maelstrom. Neighborhoods existed; permanence did not. Most of the city lived in boardinghouses, families included, and everyone picked up and moved on May 1. In the middle of all this, Whitman saw that everyone who lives in a place leaves something vital in its bricks that's lost forever when it's torn down; not just memories but pieces of the city's soul. Walt loved nothing more than he loved loving, and that included buildings. "Good-bye, old houses!" he exclaimed. "There was that about ye which I hold it no shame to say I loved passing well." His essay, though, modern as it feels, railed against something we now hold dear about New York, how it tore down and built over again to make room for millions of immigrants. It's hard to contain multitudes without growing and changing.

And change New York must. Everyone's New York dies eventually, and then, if they want, they can have a new one. For four hundred years, the only thing as strong as the city's despair has been its optimism, every leap in its progress an escape from collapse. Over and over there have been horizon events that wise pundits have called the end of New York, and over and over the city roars forward.

Until now. Maybe it's collective PTSD. We lost more than 30,000 fellow New Yorkers in those months of Covid, family, friends, and neighbors, a staggering loss that we don't talk about enough. Maybe we feel burnt by the last few bounce-backs: the redevelopment of Ground Zero went from hallowed civic duty to black hole, and the great gift of the financial crisis in 2008 was Hudson Yards. Either way, the subways are filling up again. Crime is down. Babies born, deposits paid, novels started. We want things to change, but . . . we don't want them to be that much different, either. We want to move forward, but forward into what? What does "forward" mean in New York when a growing number of people believe the Earth is flat? Many aspects of our culture are still seized up with what Kurt Andersen called "mass nostalgia": wearing, watching, and listening to things that are simply new takes on what we were wearing, watching, and listening to thirty years ago. But even when we tamed, perfected, bottled, and sold it to the world under Bloomberg, New York has never been a final product. "Most cities are nouns," said John F. Kennedy. "New York is a verb." The arrival of the supertalls was at least a provocation, a reminder that we couldn't stop time, that we had to keep moving into the future. The bad news is that, unless you're an oligarch looking down from Billionaires Row, that future looks tentative if not out-and-out scary. Faced with the prospect of climate change, rent hikes, and a politics that we can at best call perilous, the rest of us burrow into our identities, affinities, and portfolios and hope it will all take care of itself, frozen between NIMBYs and YIMBYs.

Like it or not, in the years ahead, New York City is going to become an ark. The question we need to ask ourselves is, what exactly about New York City are we going to save and what will we bring into the future? Almost two hundred years after Walt Whitman wrote his essay and most every building he knew came down, he would still recognize this city. New York is still New York—loud and crowded, diverse, super-charged, welcoming, always in search of the new, famous as far back as the early 1700s for people who talked fast and interrupted. Throw greedy, cruel, and vain in there, too.

As we enter a very, *very* uncertain future, the challenge won't be preserving buildings in New York City. It will be preserving how we live here, our values, how we defend expression and push limits; the freedom and respect we accord each other as we rub shoulders on the subway and try not to hear our neighbors through the common wall. It's our turn, and our responsibility, to demand and plan a future, a bright one, for New York and everyone in it. Everyone. We will need to save our past without making it seem that our best is behind us, and fix our mistakes always believing that something new and better is possible. Treading water and tweaking the system won't take us there. Sandbags and basement apartments aren't solutions. New York needs vision. It needs to aim somewhere. We are each of us somehow taking New York to its next place. We need to recognize that and celebrate that.

What follows are things we need to tear down and build over again to make New York ready, to make it healthy and prosperous for our children and grandchildren and the millions who will come from every nation on Earth looking for a free space to speak their language and live as they would.

Some are pipe dreams. Maybe a lot of them are. But what will really kill New York is the cynical savvy fobbed off these days as expertise. So let's dream.

New things are not exempt. For symbolic reasons, let's start with the Vessel at Hudson Yards and Little Island, both created by Thomas Heatherwick at a cost of nearly $500 million. Half. A. Billion. Dollars. If we—rightly—took down the statue of Teddy Roosevelt in front of the American Museum of Natural History as an expression of the racism, colonialism, and exploitation underpinning its collections, then these two need to come down as garish expressions of an era that tried to turn New York into some combination of Orlando and Dubai. As far back as the 1820s, when merchants from the South began coming to buy goods, cool off, and see the sights, tourism has been central to New York's economy. It now employs most of the unskilled workers who once found jobs in small manufacturing; hotels produce hundreds of millions in tax revenue. As much as New Yorkers enjoy bitching about tourists and trampling over them on the sidewalk, we know they're a necessary part of the deal and will even on occasion point them in the right direction. But tearing down Little Island and the Vessel would send the message that we're tearing up the mistaken priority of serving tourists before we proudly serve each other. Tourists come to New York to be a part of us, to live for a while in wonder of this hive of imperfect humanity constantly, energetically, and (mostly) peaceably getting on with it the way they want to get it on; to see the buildings we live and work in, the parks we play in, the places we eat, the shows we see; to experience what is unique about everyday life in this city. Little Island, notwithstanding its recent attempts at artistic relevance, has more in common with Tom Sawyer Island at Disney World than anything in New York. The Vessel is an Escher nightmare come to life, poorly conceived and ugly beyond words. These are fake destinations. In this case, we don't need to build over again; we'll be better off with them simply gone.

Making us feel safe again means we must go through with tearing down Rikers and building new borough jails. It's the law and it's supposed to happen by 2027. The next New York must be built on justice and safety *for all*, and that requires a just and fair criminal justice system that includes among

The Vessel at Hudson Yards, temporarily closed for safety reasons, opened in 2016.
It rises 16 stories and consists of 154 interconnected flights of stairs, nearly 2,500 steps,
and 80 landings that visitors could climb. PHOTO: JEFF GOLDBERG/ESTO.

its tools incarceration, but without the likelihood of abuse and the possibility of death. If we truly care about crime, about safe streets and homelessness, about better lives and second chances, then we need to start here. Tear down Rikers and develop the island's 400 or so acres into a new community, a new Roosevelt Island, Co-op City, or Stuy Town. The new New York can't afford to waste so many acres, and so many lives. (And, by the way, those unlicensed pot shops aren't helping anyone. . . .)

The third is heresy, but it brings us to our biggest problem. We need to stop talking about Robert Moses and Jane Jacobs. Neither one has solutions for the malaise we've sunk into because the problem they confronted, the solutions they offered, their means and their ends, all centered on the pleasures and terrors of one twentieth-century technology: the car. Regional planning, the exodus to the suburbs and the return, traffic, transit, zoning, gentrification, the entire postwar commuter model—they're all in some ways about cars in the city and the fact that state leadership won't support Congestion Pricing shows just how deeply we remain in their thrall (and just how much we need some leadership right now). But cars aren't the whole problem, or even the heart of it anymore. Cars aren't keeping workers from coming in to the office, or hollowing out retail. That our streets are choked with delivery trucks and the entire cab system is shot isn't about trucks or cabs. The dominant, transformative technology in New York now is the Internet, and we've embraced it with the same blind infatuation and lack of caution with which we once embraced the car.

Moses could only dream of the way the Internet has crashed through the city, driving a great big virtual LOMEX through the culture, economy, and structures of New York. It's this generation's inevitable force, the thing we can't do without because we've made it that way. Can great things be done with it? Obviously, just as cars get us to the hospital fast. But Tech also continues the anti-urban work of the car; they both atomize us, pull us apart, turn the face-to-face human exchanges that Holly Whyte identified as the essential purpose of the city into frictionless transactions. Even before Covid forced the issue, the Internet had changed how we eat, drink, buy, sell, learn, work, and have sex; we're advertised to, surveilled, influenced, and policed with it. For all the good and obvious arguments for making broadband available everywhere to everyone, it feels increasingly like a new version of paving paradise.

Should we block the Internet, like Bhutan? We couldn't even if we wanted to, and we don't. Whatever the new New York is, it will involve Tech. It should involve Tech. But as we plan and build it, we need to ask the kinds of questions we didn't ask when cars were taking over America, questions about what we *should* do versus what we *can* do, questions about misuse and abuse, and confusing convenience with quality of life. Everyone should still read *The Power Broker* and *The Death and Life of Great American Cities*, but then pick up Shoshana Zuboff's *Age of Surveillance Capitalism* and ask what it means in the city of Wall Street, or Sarah Brayne's *Predict and Surveil*, about predictive policing and the LAPD, and ask what the next Kelly or Kerik will do with that. And I haven't even mentioned AI.

The question of coming back to the office, of work and home and commercial real estate, is ultimately about the Internet sanding away the daily grit of urban life—Vishaan Chakrabarti calls it "social friction." Now, it's great for life to be as convenient as you can possibly make it, to get exactly what you want when you want it, without questions, without getting your hands dirty—and free shipping, too! To see only what you want to see and hear only what you want to hear. But we've traded shared space for a million tiny worlds existing next to each other. Every man his own suburb! Covid didn't start this process; it just sped it up with a substitute way of living that we're now convinced is the *only* way to live. Machines are made for pure information, but meaning in the city depends on that friction. Love, duty, empathy, care, connection—the things that make communities—all come out of the static of daily interactions, and they're still the reason people come to New York—for contact, exchange, and the heat of shared humanity. Tearing down and building over again for the New York ahead means restoring chances for encountering others.

We've done this work before. Breaking down old zoning silos for

Empty Midtown offices reflect the impact of the 2020 to 2023 Covid pandemic, which diminished the vibrancy of this once-bustling area. PHOTO: ASHLEY GILBERTSON.

mixed-use districts was crucial to New York's post–fiscal crisis resuscitation. From Fluxus and Yoko to Loft Laws and Landmarks, SoHo was about creating new opportunities for urban friction. More recently, converting commercial to residential in the oldest part of the city pumped new life into the Financial District. So what we're really talking about when we talk about the life and death of the commercial business district is Midtown. That makes sense, because for all its glass and stone and steel, Midtown *is* a living thing. It's never finished, nor has it ever been some ideal of what central business districts are supposed to be. We've tinkered with it in the past, and now it's time again to dream up some new plans and dramatic interventions that account for residential life. Let's take back the windswept plazas and enervating water features plashing on Sixth Avenue, Holly Whyte's ideas warped into corporate tradeoffs, and turn it into a leafy boulevard connecting Bryant Park and Central Park. Could we take that south down to Herald Square and Penn South? Why not? What if Penn South wasn't just another collection of supertalls around a new arena—with all the horrible echoes of Atlantic Yards that brings—but an actual place? Tennis courts might look like a silly idea (and they are), but the ranch houses in the South Bronx were a silly idea, too, and they woke people up to new possibilities. What about a park, or a plaza constantly activated by all the uses of Penn Station and Madison Square Garden? And please, please, let's build a new Penn Station.

Reuse and repurpose are the gold standard, and conversion from commercial to residential is terrific, but it's clear already that they're too expensive and too complicated to solve everything. We can't just swap out desks for bedroom sets; the different codes on details like windows and plumbing often require a complete redesign and moving fundamental physical systems. Ironically, some of the best candidates for conversion are the oldest. Pre-war office buildings are closer to residential layouts, so there might be a silver lining to the fact that New York's building stock is surprisingly old—as of 2019, the average age of a Manhattan office building was seventy-seven years, and ninety-seven in Midtown South. But while a well-maintained and well-designed tall building can last for centuries, not all of them are. If a building can't be reused or repurposed, if it's standing empty on someone's books as a write-off, if its only argument for existence is that it exists, let's tear it down.

What we need to build in their place, though, aren't casinos. We need to build neighborhoods. Live/work communities that blend different incomes, different ages, and different sizes of households, that bring day-to-day workers flowing through the roots of those who live there. Battery Park City created a community. It's its own place, Battery Park City, a step to the side of what's going on around it and legally the property of New York State. Yes, that brings complications. Yes, it's anomalous in many ways. But it works as both a place of business and home for thousands of New Yorkers, not all of whom are luxury condo owners. The tourist gimmicks and luxury retail are there, but they're not there just to serve luxury visitors. The best housing plans in New York's history, from the first Amalgamated co-ops in the Bronx to Nehemiah Housing and the whole Koch-era initiative, weren't created by the marketplace alone, or the government. They were created by public/private partnerships, and by communities, unions, and faith groups. If we're going to do transformational things, it makes sense to partner with organizations that provide community off the shelf.

To really get anything truly transformative done will mean tearing up how we deal with zoning and land use. The Uniform Land Use Review Procedure (ULURP) is a good thing. Started in 1975, it requires land use plans to go before community boards, the relevant borough president, the City Planning Commission, the City Council, and then the mayor, but the council has the final say and can override their veto. We don't need to tear up ULURP. But we do need to tear up council member deference. Right now, any one council member can effectively shoot down a plan sited in their district no matter its merits, no matter its benefit to the city at large by claiming that it goes against the community's interests. It's not a law—it's council etiquette and it hurts New York. While on the one hand deference sounds like a way to keep City Hall from bullying communities, it also prevents large-scale, long-term, comprehensive planning and keeps the city from delivering the full weight of what it can do, effectively and at the scale that can really make a difference. If a council member has good reasons to block a project, they should be able to convince enough of their colleagues to agree.

Now let's talk about the New York City Housing Authority (NYCHA). Someone has to. Some 360,000 New Yorkers live in some 2,400 NYCHA buildings that were built cheaply in the first place and have been run to the ground since by federal defunding, corrupt officials, neglectful tenants, lazy workers, and mayor after mayor who's seen nothing in it for them to pay much attention. While private companies don't seem to be doing any better than NYCHA at caring for NYCHA housing, the city's lack of interest in really changing anything, even in the face of recent corruption scandals, means we have to entertain big ideas like the plans for the Robert Fulton Houses in Chelsea, which will literally tear it all down and build over again, with housing guaranteed for all current residents within a new mixed-use, mixed-income development. If City Hall had the will to actually make NYCHA function, it would mean tearing the whole thing down to the studs anyway. Let's think fresh. Projects like Via Verde in the Bronx show that better things are possible, but the status quo now means letting it all fall apart, taking those 360,000 New Yorkers down with it.

One "community" that needs to be involved in every step here is the real estate "community," though today that stretches any geographical definition of the term. New York's real estate is globally owned. The trade-off of the grid back in 1811 was that the city's one natural resource would be packaged up and commodified, and we would tax all the proceeds. But what sounds like common sense hid the imbalance—we would always depend on real estate owners to pay our bills, so anything that hurts the real estate market hurts the entire city, even when "hurting" it with lower values and lower rents is exactly what the city needs. With this logic, we've been convinced to accept that the wild chasm of inequity is the very thing that makes a functional New York possible, when the reality is that some of the most generative, forward-looking moments in New York's history have started during real estate busts, when for some tiny window we could imagine something more for the land

The residential development Via Verde (2012) by Dattner Architects provides affordable, sustainable urban living in the South Bronx, and was the winning entry in the New Housing New York Legacy Competition.
PHOTO: DAVID SUNDBERG/ESTO; COURTESY OF PHIPPS/ROSE/ DATTNER/GRIMSHAW.

than just maximum price per square foot. What we don't need during a real estate crisis that somehow also manages to produce record sales are city programs that slap new lipstick on low-end office buildings.

All these questions of density and housing and growth aren't just about Manhattan; not everyone can live in a sparkling new futuristic mixed-use development, nor does everyone want to, and mid-block sliver buildings on the Upper East Side were, and remain, a terrible idea. One of the most surprising and most positive aspects of the city's post–fiscal crisis transformation was how the popular understanding of New York changed from Manhattan and four outer boroughs to a single place at once bigger and more populated but also more intimate, where *all* the boroughs repped New York in their own ways. It's helped us make space for immigrants and new cultures, and it's how we can make more space for those still coming. This isn't just a matter of housing. It's been a while since Manhattan was the primary landing space for newcomers. We need to build up incrementally in low-density areas throughout the city, not just for housing, but to create spaces where we can engage and cultivate healthy communities, old and new, that in turn enrich the rest of the city. Both the City of Yes program and Practice for Architecture and Urbanism | PAU's Affordable New York, or One Million plan, offer approaches that we as a city should rally around. The Koch-era housing initiative made New York's rebirth possible not only in terms of tax revenue but also in how we lived together. Fingers crossed that the state budget deal of 2024 offered enough to get the city building again, and City of Yes survives ULURP.

Tomasi di Lampedusa's novel *The Leopard* takes place during Whitman's time, at another moment of upheaval and transformation. Though the upstart Prince Tancredi is talking about Sicily, what he says is maybe closer to what we need to hear than anything Walt said. "For things to remain the same," says Prince Tancredi, "everything has to change." If the new New York is to be a New York that we will know, that Walt Whitman would know, a city full of people, full of noise, full of diversity, freedom, expression, and exchange, we will need to constantly examine our buildings, structures, and institutions and be willing to tear down and build over again. 🏛

St. Ann's Warehouse, a performing arts institution in Brooklyn Bridge Park, was originally the Tobacco Warehouse (1860); in 2015, Marvel Architects adapted it for its new use. PHOTO: DAVID SUNDBERG/ESTO.

JUSTIN DAVIDSON

THE LONG VIEW:
BUILDING FOR REBUILDING

NEW YORK, like cities all over the world, has spent decades combing through the architectural detritus of industry, salvaging buildings that have outlived their purpose. We no longer need so many waterside factories to churn out paper and pianos or refineries to spin molasses into sugar. We can do without warehouses like the one a *Harper's* reporter toured in 1877 and found "rows of dusty white barrels of China clay stand[ing] alongside rows of barrels of plumbago from Ceylon, whose black dust makes the floor all about as slippery as glass." But all the moving and making and fixing and processing that once powered New York's economy—the coal-smoke-tainted, sweat-drenched enterprises of the nineteenth and twenti-eth centuries—left us with a scattering of silent shells that turn out to be perfectly adapted to the twenty-first century's more sedentary needs. And so, in Hudson Square, an elevated railway station got sheared off, stripped down, and extended into a Google nerve center (by CookFox). In Harlem, a multistory windowless storage facility, part of a long-abandoned brewery complex, metamorphosed into an art gallery attached to offices (thanks to Gluck+). At Manhattan's southern tip, a graceful ferry terminal was re-born as a private club (Marvel). In Brooklyn, the shell of a tobacco ware-house was repurposed as a theater (Marvel again). Even the computer age has its abandoned hulks: Manufacturers Hanover Trust's glowering data

Gluck+ expanded this early twentieth-century warehouse block in Harlem for mixed-use development in 2023. The original buildings were preserved; new construction, clearly distinguished from the original, was placed above the historic fabric. PHOTO: GLUCK +.

processing center from the 1960s is being hollowed out, aerated, and converted into apartments (CetraRuddy).

New Yorkers should be grateful for the way those old skeletons absorb the blows of refurbishment. With mute patience, they perform tasks they were never meant for, and when they're done with those, they stand ready to do yet other jobs that haven't been invented yet. There's a lesson in that history. If an old building is to survive, it must prove itself useful even after it's been declared obsolete. That conclusion seems so obvious when we survey the past, yet so puzzling when we look to the future. Any architect or developer who opens a new building in 2025 should want it to keep serving society's changing needs, to earn its place on the land it occupies, stand as a reminder of our time, and spare the environment the havoc wrought by knocking it down. It's not just vainglory that might inspire architects to make buildings that could last for centuries; they should want to contribute to cultural continuity rather than participate in a process of constant erasure. A good building should be ready for the unavoidably unpredictable future, and we've seen that the key is versatility. Which raises some brow-furrowing questions: How do you plan for unknown contingencies? What would it mean to create a building that stakes a claim to its own preservation? How can architects in the 2020s give their new structures the best shot at another life once the first has run its course?

As a society, we rarely bother to try. New commercial architecture has a limited lifespan, by design. By the time an office building is fifty years old, it's looking ready for retirement. At seventy, it might as well be dead. Architecture that sticks around beyond those birthdays does so mostly by neglect and occasionally by statute, if it's important enough. The recent renovation of Lever House by Skidmore, Owings & Merrill (SOM) has turned the firm's own formerly cutting-edge, presumptively short-lived masterwork into a (ravishing) museum version of itself. It survives on prestige alone.

Thoughts of posterity play no role in the ordinary course of refreshing the cityscape. The habits of development, the pathways of financing, the global supply chain, and the conventions of the construction industry are all organized to produce a built environment designed to be torn down—soon. Lenders want budgets to be frugal. Value engineers are assigned to keep them that way. Prefabricated products come with fixed-term warranties and built-in expiration dates. Curtain walls fail. Façade panels degrade. Advanced electronics are almost immediately obsolete. Buildings are crammed with preordained debris, most of it the construction industry's equivalent of supermarket plastic bags: useless but eternal. Archaeologists will be digging up shards of our disposable buildings for millennia, wondering why we insisted on elements that aged quickly yet never decomposed. Plenty of designers have experience reviving architecture that was never intended to last. Firms like CetraRuddy, now engaged in converting abandoned office towers from the second half of the twentieth century into massive apartment complexes, are learning how to rescue buildings that have passed their sell-by date and leached away most of their value. Their colleagues a couple of generations from now will have to contend with an ever-vaster trove of superannuated structures, and they will find their task made thornier by designs that were so obsessed with efficiency and specificity that they're not prepared for a second life.

Today's busiest architects are those who can satisfy a client's rundown of requirements with dexterity and finesse, tailoring spaces to purposes that won't mean a thing a couple of generations from now. The largest and most expensive projects grapple with the most complex and specialized needs: humidity control in museums, ultra-high-speed connectivity for financial institutions, blast-resistant walls in government buildings, golf simulators in high-end condos, vibration dampening in research labs, and sound isolation in theaters and concert halls. And yet if there's one brutal lesson of today's sudden office-space glut, it's that obsolescence can arrive at frightening speed. I'm not all that ancient yet, but whole categories that formed the cityscape of my youth are now all but gone: urban stables, military installations, phone boxes, tollbooths, printing plants, newsstands. Department stores and shopping malls are thinning out. I suspect that before too long we'll discover we no longer have much use for trading floors, E-sports arenas, IMAX movie theaters, or television sound stages. If these structures can't serve another round of needs, they will all be abandoned and then plowed into landfill. Think of flexibility as the social equivalent of flood insurance: when that trendy, highly specialized business goes under, property owners should be ready to retool.

(As a side note, my focus here is on commercial buildings, but similar arguments apply to some residential architecture—especially the abodes of the super-rich, which have historically been turned over to less exclusive uses.

Palaces, villas, and mansions become museums, embassies, and schools. Now try to imagine repurposing the diamond needles along 57th Street when they eventually lose their oligarch cachet. Everything that makes them valuable as deluxe residences—floor-to-ceiling windows, private elevators, intelligent but delicate climate control, suites of walk-in closets, and so on—would turn into a headache for an institution.)

Erecting buildings in the expectation that they will one day be rebuilt demands a fresh way of thinking about architecture that is also an old way. It's a philosophy that endows existing works with the right to keep standing. In exchange, it asks that they be amenable to radical transformation.

I periodically ask architects what strategies might increase the range of options down the line. They don't always have an answer; they are trained to fulfill the requirements of those who pay them, not to meet the needs of clients who have yet to be born. Sometimes, though, they come up with deceptively straightforward solutions. Invest in quality: Buy the more expensive waterproofing that costs twice as much and lasts three times as long (courtesy of Rick Cook at CookFox). Design around a modular grid system, which can be more easily adapted than an idiosyncratic form of waves and swoops (Chris

A façade detail of one of the two side-by-side, 20-story Maverick Buildings (2022) in Chelsea, which house condominium residences. PHOTO: CHRIS COE/DXA STUDIO.

Cooper at SOM). Opt for masonry façades, which can be punched through, filled in, and patched up in ways that glass curtain walls can't (Jordan Rogove at DXA Studio). Adopt natural materials such as stone instead of highly engineered products that will eventually age into scrap. Where possible, maximize natural ventilation and daylight to reduce the need for complex mechanical and electronic systems. Design components so they are easy to disassemble. Think about how materials can eventually be recycled.

None of these proposals is revolutionary or technically challenging. Some cost more than current conventional practice. Most cut against the accumulation of habits and codes that guide the design process long before the first sketch. To take one example: New York's byzantine zoning code often makes it difficult to cram all the allowable floor area into the envelope determined by height, bulk, and setback requirements. It's like trying to pack ten pounds of potatoes into a five-pound bag. One standard approach to the conundrum is to slip as many floors as possible inside the shell, which in turn means minimizing floor-to-floor heights. In theory, it would be nice to add a couple of feet of interior headspace and get ceilings that are twelve instead of ten feet high. The problem is that, while more headroom would make interiors more comfortable and buildings more adaptable, it would almost inevitably mean sacrificing floor area. I can hear developers scream: Square footage is money! No sane businessperson would relinquish so much as a square inch of New York real estate, except under duress. Forget it.

Or consider another possible tweak to standard dimensions that would boost a building's versatility: modifying its thickness, especially toward the bottom. The current spate of office-to-residential conversions faces one frequently unbridgeable chasm that divides commercial from residential highrises. The largest, most desirable office tenants (banks, for instance) demand vast floor plates that yield great distances from the glassed-in edge to the dark inner regions where the supply closets are and the lowliest employees dwell. Apartments, on the other hand, must maximize daylight and views, which keeps the floor area small and the distance from façade to front door relatively short. The difference creates a bifurcated skyline of fat office sky-

THE LONG VIEW: BUILDING FOR REBUILDING

scrapers and skinny or slablike apartment towers. That's fine so long as the need for both remains robust, but inflexible dimensions (and outdated zoning regulations) make it virtually impossible to fit work and life into the same container. With rare exceptions, mixed-use towers are not a New York thing. Sure, architects could propose compromises to adequately, if not ideally, serve multiple purposes, but their clients would briskly turn them down with an unanswerable dismissal: *That's not how we do things.*

You might think that the long view should be the norm in the real estate industry, where projects take years to realize and revenues trickle in over decades. In practice, few developers, as they start gathering the billion or two it takes to put up a major new addition to the skyline, want to start off by accepting a less than ideal solution to their current needs on the off chance that someone else will have different requirements sometime in the future. Builders ask for the heights, depths, floor areas, and windows that brokers tell them they can sell or rent with the highest possible return—right now. And so the conversation about the future stalls, and architects, certain of rejection, refrain from even suggesting common-sense techniques to increase a building's life expectancy.

Convention is a powerful force, honored in history, enshrined in law, reinforced by repetition, and subject to change only through constant, unstoppable pressure. Beach houses can't withstand coastal flooding, but convention can, and so they keep getting rebuilt. And convention routinely shuts out foresight. The mismatch between tradition and projection is particularly glaring when it comes to parking. Car-owning residents of most cities and suburbs have historically believed there's no such thing as enough space for idle vehicles in their neighborhoods. They've insisted that all new buildings provide their own, so as not to ratchet up competition for on-street parking. Consequently, developers are often obliged to erect bigger and more expensive garages than they need, a discrepancy that can be catastrophic. The new Yankee Stadium that opened in 2009 came with enough space for 9,300 cars. Instead of driving, fans wisely took advantage of the subway stop a block away, and the facility stood empty, eventually defaulting on the municipal bonds that had been issued to build it. Which leaves the Bronx with a set of useless, money-sucking megastructures that are probably destined to be torn down.

It's a shame that the Yankees didn't take inspiration from the Kent Automatic Garage, which opened at Columbus Avenue and West 61st Street in 1929, using an "electric parking machine" and a freight elevator to jigsaw 1,000 cars into 24 stories. In 1943, it was turned into a storage facility for other kinds of possessions. Now it's a high-rise condo joined with a Fordham University academic building. These days, the rate of car ownership is in flux again. It dropped for a while, as millennials postponed getting their licenses, then got nudged higher by the pandemic-induced fear of public transportation. It's impossible to predict whether our great-grandchildren will drive less and own fewer cars, ride in shared driverless robots, or cram ever wider highways with ever more vehicles. Will we need ever more spaces or almost none? That uncertainty should lead builders everywhere to plan parking structures that can adapt to a range of cultural shifts. Fortunately, multistory white elephant parking structures can be retooled as apartments, though only if they have flat floors and speed ramps rather than continuous corkscrews.

The stories of those two parking garages, opened nearly a century apart, can be read as a fable with a ringing moral: Make buildings nimble. Instead, the business of erecting cities operates by a different commandment: Make buildings efficient. That term, which has acquired a kind of majestic infallibility, has an assortment of different meanings. Modernism lends it an aesthetic dimension: the purity of seamless surfaces and clean lines. The cost of materials makes it a financial principle: Spend only what you must. Climate change elevates efficiency to an environmental virtue: the imperative to burn and emit as little as possible. These various rationales add up to the same approach, especially in the most high-design, high-tech high-rises. Squeeze out every last drib of space, pare back energy costs, and whittle down every extra pound of concrete and steel until your design is as lean as a racehorse. The environmental argument is an especially irresistible one, because it's rooted not in subjective aesthetic judgments or in a private company's balance sheet but in the facts of collective crisis. Manufacturing concrete and steel contributes about 16 percent of the world's emissions; the more you use, the more harm you do. Sophisticated software makes it possible to quantify the efficiency of trusses, columns, and floor slabs with astonishing precision. Architects and engineers can use it to tweak a structure or account for mutable wind currents and the probability of tremors. Computers can also help adjust the budget for variations in design. You want to know how much you could save by cutting one bathroom stall per floor and what the consequent wait times would be? Done.

Such an abundance of data makes it a sin to pad a building with any more load-bearing capacity than it needs. The flip side of that argument, though, is this: the only thing more damaging to the planet than putting up a new building is tearing down an old one and replacing it with another. Demolition dissipates all the energy that's packed into a building's mass. Shattering floor slabs, melting down girders, trucking away rubble, excavating new foundations, erecting a whole structure—it all eats away at the atmosphere. "Demolishing is a decision of easiness and short term," the Pritzker Prize–winning French architect Anne Lacaton has said. "It is a waste of many things—a waste of energy, a waste of material, and a waste of history. Moreover, it has a very negative social impact. For us, it is an act of violence."

The commandment that Lacaton implied—*Never demolish!*—suggests a corollary: Every new building should be responsible for postponing its own demolition as long as possible. That would mean designing a superstructure robust and flexible enough that it can one day carry more weight, shift loads laterally, and be strategically cut away or added onto as needs change. Our generation can reuse nineteenth- and early-twentieth-century structures because, by today's standards, they were extravagantly built. Engineers had to estimate loads and tensile strength, and so they erred on the side of caution, beefing up bridges so much that for many years we could blithely neglect to maintain them; they just kept soldiering on. Industrial-age builders kitted out their world with faith in the long term, and later generations kept fixing up the holdovers, wearing them down, and fixing them up again. St. John's Terminal, the 1930s rail facility on the West Side of Manhattan that

The St. John's Terminal, a 1930s railway terminal, once served as an endpoint to the rail line now known as the High Line. It was adapted by CookFox and Gensler for Google's New York City headquarters. PHOTO: GOOGLE.

was designed to receive freight trains on a raised track, now supports eight floors of new Google offices, thanks to a design by CookFox and Gensler. That example, like countless others, leads to a counterintuitive conclusion: maybe it makes sense to pollute a bit more now so as to pollute a lot less later.

The provisional list of measures I've laid out to promote adaptability—higher ceilings, masonry walls, moderate floor plates, modular design, and robust structure—might appear to imply that long-lived buildings must be stolid and generic, or that the future will find use only for clunky, thick-walled workhorses that are too much trouble to take down. But history tells us that there's an aesthetic dimension to longevity, too. The most potent force for preservation is beauty. Would-be slate-wipers find it hard to demolish a structure if enough people love it, even when it isn't protected by law. In contemporary adaptive reuse projects, architects go to great lengths to keep elaborate ornaments, idiosyncratic attics, elegant staircases, and unreproducible details. The awesome size and sheer bulk of industrial-age relics can make for exciting spaces, especially when designs shaped by one era's needs slip seamlessly into the next. The contemporary art museum Dia Beacon, for instance, occupies a box plant with a sawtooth roofline equipped with skylights that once poured shadowless daylight onto the factory floor and now provides the perfect luminescence for minimalist sculpture. In other projects, defunct essentials like smokestacks get demoted to evocative ornaments, as at the Domino Sugar Refinery in Williamsburg. In both cases, those buildings survived their original purpose in part because the design had value.

We can't predict what future generations will value, but today's architects should at least *try* to seduce the preservationists of, say 2100, into according their work due respect. That doesn't mean just peppering the planet with flamboyant one-off masterpieces à la Guggenheim Bilbao, but imbuing our useful, workaday buildings with spirit and character, making them better than they strictly need to be. In some quarters, preservation is thought of as an antiquarian undertaking, a sentimental allegiance to structures that have ceased to function and so have relinquished their right to exist. The same sort of thinking applies to new buildings, where architectural goals like sensuality, elegance, texture, proportion, and personality get dismissed as aesthetic frills, options that might be added (contingent on budget) once the problems of handling water, waste, and crowds have been taken care of. And yet these two aspects of our built environment—reuse and refinement—are essential guarantors of continuity, protectors of memory, and hedges against climactic degradation. Wise people plan for the aging of their bodies. A wise society should plan for the aging of its physical plant, too. ᛘ

Eero Saarinen designed the Trans World Airlines (TWA) Flight Center (1962) at the
John F. Kennedy International Airport in Queens with a futuristic reinforced-concrete
roof resembling two wings, to convey the sensation of flight and the excitement of travel.
The Flight Center is now a hotel. PHOTO: EZRA STOLLER/ESTO.

VISHAAN CHAKRABARTI

PRESERVING THE FUTURE:
ARCHITECTURE AS ARCHAEOLOGY

WHEN RIGOROUSLY CONCEIVED, preservation provides hope for the future. Sound preservation creates a horizon toward which history marches, a future that is inextricably enmeshed with the past. But the future barely lives—the planet burns, wars rage, mental health declines, democracy's heartbeat flutters, all while algorithms learn. The future barely lives.

Imagine then, at this precarious historical moment, speaking to the next generation, to my children, to anyone's children, about the significance of architecture and preservation. Most would laugh ruthlessly at the seeming irrelevance. The joy of childhood wonders—like my young love of cities—would be quashed mercilessly by the jeer of cynicism. Other than some jabber about the occasional "green" building in a suburban parking lot, what hope does our built environment offer to this pageant of pessimism?

To this, my only response can be that, for humanity, little exists "beyond architecture." From the primitive hut to the International Space Station, architecture surrounds us, protects us, and, despite some notable exceptions, differentiates us as a species. Like air, water, love, and hope, we need architecture, we are defined by it, and we largely ignore it.

Tired approaches from the twentieth century provide us the wrong frame to argue for the future, to argue for hope. Historic versus modern buildings.

Old cities versus new. Preservationists versus developers. Brick versus glass. The binaries themselves are irrelevant because they reflect little of our condition—they only serve to fuel the pessimism. They are battles in a rearview mirror, a window into a foregone era when the combatants enjoyed dividends of peace and privilege long since depleted.

Could there be a different, nonbinary, time-fluid frame through which to assess and argue for architecture, its ability to last, and its inarguable relevance to a world on fire? Few blocks of urban fabric, and even fewer pieces of architecture, have the power to convey simultaneously what was, what is, and what can be. That rare triad—the ability of architecture to be a window into our past, a mirror of the present, and a periscope into the future—is what makes the Parthenon, the Hagia Sophia, or Eero Saarinen's TWA terminal worthy of our enduring love. Conceived as one thing yet used as another, these structures stand the test of time in ways most buildings would envy if they could.

Imagine if Midtown Manhattan's Third and Sixth Avenues could bend with time instead of break with obsolescence? In all the conversations we hear today about converting vacant office buildings to residential—most of which are impossible or unwise to convert because of their large floors, low ceilings, and forests of columns—little is discussed about how our building stock became so inflexible in the first place, how it devolved owing to the specialist demands of corporate finance and cookie-cutter real estate. The monied development experts, who swan among us like the gods of Gotham . . . they couldn't possibly have gotten it wrong—could they have? As we know in Manhattan, the rich are *never* wrong! Yet consider what great shape New York would be in, if Midtown's older office stock had been primarily built out of the typology of SoHo's flexible lofts instead of Emery Roth's ever static, thinly layered wedding cakes. Imagine if we had listened to the metabolists and Archigram more than, or at least as much as, the cohort of billionaires who to this minute control most of our city's urban fabric.

The longevity we seek is also evident in most good urban housing, as opposed to most suburban sprawl, in the sense that its beat goes on decade upon decade, century upon century. Our white brick apartment blocks and brownstones, our ruddy row houses, with their illegal walk-ups and shadowy light shafts, all embody not only the energy it took to build them, but also the multitudes of narratives they contain, the capacity they still yield for the future of culture. Having sheltered waves of immigrants from countries and colleges, New York's tenement neighborhoods remain dense and vibrant post-pandemic, as do I. M. Pei's Kips Bay and Davis, Brody, and Bond's Waterside Plaza. They persevere because we persevere in them. But in the canon of high modernist architecture, these examples are perhaps the outliers.

The fathers of modernism, much louder than its mothers (like the quiet "houser" Catherine Bauer Wurster), insisted they had broken the chain. Tabula rasa! Out with the old, in with the new, even if much of it had the shelf life of sushi, born as it was from the luminescent but ephemeral language of the shoji screen. From the blood, ash, and smoke of two world wars emerged the understandable urge to reinvent, to experiment, and, less understandably, to fulfill Le Corbusier's dream of killing the street. Many of those early modern projects were like the Ise Shrine, there for use, demolition, and rebirth, rather than reuse. Mies van der Rohe's Barcelona Pavilion was not about use; it was about space and time, about the relative, uncertain nature of existence revealed by twentieth-century physics. Even Le Corbusier's raw concrete Capitol Complex at Chandigarh, India, when you experience it up close, feels temporary somehow, feels as though it will melt back into its earthen plain. It and his never-built Plan Obus, like today's far more absurd NEOM in the Saudi desert, are willful personal experiments in a brown person's land, the colonial equivalent of donning a sombrero, downing the shot, and devouring the worm soon after you lock your Chevy in Tijuana's sun.

Louis Kahn was the exception among his peers, a modernist architect and musician who insisted on looking backward to move forward, insisted that

The Kips Bay Towers complex (1965), designed by I. M. Pei in the brutalist style with a distinctive cast-in-place concrete façade, houses condominium apartments and a 3-acre garden.
PHOTO: VICTOR ORLEWICZ; COURTESY ZBIGNIEW ORLEWICZ.

his work be wedded to time. His Sher-e-Bangla Nagar was conceived as the Capitol Complex for East Pakistan only for it to transform into the epicenter of Bangladeshi government by its completion almost two decades later. Next door and into the next century, Prime Minister Narendra Modi, architect of the denouement of an India born as secular, is now on a march to demolish the monuments of that secularism, including masterworks by Kahn, and, in some cases, to replace them with structures of Hindu cultural domination through the weaponization of history. Perhaps his shakier hold on power during his third term will shake his obsessions in this regard. Such are the horrifying risks of preserving history in amber, because it always begs the questions of whose history and whose amber. Albert Speer's neoclassicism was no accident, nor is Donald Trump's love of the same. This is not the fault of neoclassicism, but rather that of the fools who imagine it to be the epitome of the West's dominant culture.

We have no dominant culture today in the West, much to the chagrin of some and the cheer of others. The parents of modernism are dead, and we, their children and grandchildren, are a churlish, fickle, and often hapless bunch. We struggle to preserve their work. Wright and Rudolph houses flap in the wind. Brutalism struggles to find meaning and a larger fan base. Post-modernists seek solace in historicism and irony, but an obsolete office building with a fat pyramid top is no less obsolete than a modernist box. Heavy is the head that wears such an unwieldy crown.

How, then, to forge a path forward that maps the road behind while also marking *you are here,* and how do we imagine, with all there is to be despondent about in this world, that this is a pressing question for future generations, given the truly existential struggles they face?

If the binaries of the past no longer serve us, perhaps the nonbinaries of the present offer more promise. The easy analogy is with contemporary gender discourse, which immerses us in the ideas of the fluid and the nonbinary. More subtle but just as prevalent among the young is a complete rejection of racial and cultural identity that is not self-assigned. For them, the very assumption of category is the cardinal sin—they, in a supreme, game-changing act of personal agency, insist upon defining who they are in the world themselves, whether it be in terms of race, gender, sexuality, or occupation, instead of having the assumptions of others impose these characteristics upon them through guesswork and laziness. For we of gray hair and furrowed brow who find all this focus upon agency to be self-indulgent or worse, we need to "snap out of it," as Cher declared in *Moonstruck.* Wherever fluidity may lead, it's not going to evaporate. We must swim in it.

What then if our conceptions of architecture, its use and meaning over time, were, like our young friends, much more fluid? This idea is not entirely new even within the rigors of modernist thought. Heretical mid-century architect Aldo van Eyck famously stated that "whatever space and time mean, place and occasion mean more," which was essentially a rhetorical diss of Sigfried Giedion's focus on the abstract, objective, epistemological idea of space and time in favor of a more grounded, conditional, ontological understanding of our built environment as drawing meaning through its use and experience.[1] This argument for the subjective is at the heart of the postmodern critique, of course, but in architecture this valid critique quickly gave way to the cynical constructs of style, including historicism, pastiche, and irony. (Think buildings, ahem, shaped like binoculars.)

But if we stay with the baby of the critique rather than the bathwater of how it was made manifest, we take a different journey. That path passes through theorist and historian Kenneth Frampton's "Towards a Critical Regionalism," which argued for a more place-based, context-interpretive, local modernism—a set of ideas that has gained tremendous new currency in a world struggling with the onslaught of climate change, social injustice, and banal blue glass skyscrapers consuming every major city across Asia, Europe, and the Americas.[2] It is no coincidence that we see some of the best emergent architecture from the Global South, from Diébédo Francis Kéré and Marina Tabassum to Alejandro Aravena and Tatiana Bilbao. *Vive la résistance!*

These friends and colleagues are not only architects; they are archaeologists. In different ways they reflect or reveal Frampton's ideas about conditional, place-based criticality in architecture. Famed projects like Aravena's Half a House channel van Eyck's emphasis on place and occasion by privileging the user over the designer; the work is not "beyond architecture"—it is

---

1   Aldo van Eyck, *Writings: Collected Articles and Other Writings 1947–1998*, edited by V. Ligtelijn and F. Strauven (Amsterdam: SUN Publishers, 2008), 317.

2   Kenneth Frampton, "Towards a Critical Regionalism: Six Points for an Architecture of Resistance," in *The Anti-Aesthetic: Essays on Postmodern Culture*, edited by Hal Foster, 16–30 (Port Townsend, WA: Bay Press, 1983).

"beyond the architect." This work has enormous social meaning in a world where billions are unhoused or under-housed, and it also has great architectural meaning in the sense that its identity is fluid. No style can be attached to it despite the fact that the processes that created it are unabashedly modern, tied as they are to N. John Habraken's ideas about community-built architecture and the subsequent efforts of "sites and services" to give populations in need the tools they require to build and guide their own lives.[3] The work, modest as it is, transcends history.

What do such endeavors teach those of us who practice in the Global North, driven as it is by the dual forces of extreme private capital and extreme government regulation, both of which would make this work from the Global South illegal, infeasible, or both? While such projects do not directly translate to these shores, the ethos of architect as archaeologist most certainly can. Many of our solutions are hiding in plain sight, and yet they demand the act of being unearthed.

Much of the work of my Manhattan studio, Practice for Architecture and Urbanism | PAU, attempts this archaeology, attempts to celebrate the lyricism of the existing by bridging past, present, and future. Establishing solutions for New York's Pennsylvania Station by seeking a palimpsest of old and new; working with *The New York Times* to find sites for much-needed housing, or to reimagine New York's asphalt for people instead of cars; tackling research projects that explore the "loft of the future"— buildings that could be used for offices one day, apartments the next, and classrooms the day after; designing a bridge in Indianapolis that emulates the trees on the banks of the river it spans; and building adaptive reuse projects like the Domino Sugar Refinery that fully blur the line between historic and contemporary, brick and glass, nature and city, the material and the immaterial. Today, Domino is planned for food and beverage, athletic, office, and event uses, but in the future, it could be used for culture,

---

3   John F. C. Turner, *Housing by People: Towards Autonomy in Building Environments* (London: Marion Boyars, 1976).

In 1882, Theodore A. Havemeyer, in association with Thomas Winslow and J. E. James, constructed the Domino Sugar Refinery that long dominated both Brooklyn's skyline and economy. At the start of the twentieth century, the Havemeyer family, owners of the refinery, controlled 98 percent of sugar production in the United States. In 2017, PAU began the design for the adaptive reuse of this industrial landmark. PHOTO: MAX TOUHEY.

manufacturing, or education. Today and forever the building cannot be categorized as old or new; it is a New York City landmark that lives well into the future, with a big, visible, glass barrel vault intervention that echoes the original's American round arch style, a landmark that inhabits the new and saves the old. Such is the dynamic of nonbinary preservation.

This conception of heritage is fluid in its processes and product, leading us away from simplistic questions of "was the building preserved in amber?" to "does the building, née the city, have a new life that connects past, present, and future?" More importantly, does the work from all of these architect archaeologists practicing globally represent some kind of relevance to a pessimistic, ruptured world in which our young see so little hope?

I don't know. But we can at least model a paradigm shift away from the fights of old. The world can't afford them. We can instead inspire, through example, work that grounds people in the continuum of history and the connection of people rather than the conflicts on their screens. Given our mental health crisis, I believe great cities, inviting public places, and connective architecture are the antidote to the scourge of social media. The longest study of human happiness in the world, still going on at Harvard University, finds that social connection is critical to health and happiness across all ages, genders, and ethnicities, demonstrably leading to significantly longer lifespans.[4] So let us build places for people to forge and deepen those social connections! Let us offer our disillusioned young engaging spaces to connect across cultures and time IRL, as they say, in real life! If the call of the French Revolution was "off with their heads!," the call of this revolution is "off with their phones!"

To do so, we must offer them something other than banal spaces en route from the airport until we arrive at the lavish elite spaces of downtown. If we can instead elevate the quotidian in our environment—the housing of everyday people of modest means, the quality of our streets and sidewalks, the safety and

---

4 Robert Waldinger and Marc Schulz, *The Good Life: Lessons from the World's Longest Scientific Study of Happiness* (New York: Simon & Schuster, 2023), 29, 47.

As part of the renovation of the Domino Sugar Refinery, PAU nestled a new glass building into the existing brick façade. The building reopened in 2023, with 460,000 square feet of office space, a triple-height atrium lobby, and access to the Williamsburg waterfront. PHOTO: MAX TOUHEY.

reliability of our mass transit systems, the design of our scaffolding—if we can convince our youth that we care about the constructions of our daily lives; constructions that impact all people; constructions that better our environment and connect us across time, climate, and community; constructions that bring us civic delight . . . perhaps then we will have earned some relevance; perhaps then, as a consequence of mindful building, the future has a shot at survival, and with it our hopes and dreams.

As our cities grow and grow to house our kaleidoscopic multitudes, we must build an architecture of urbanity that celebrates nature, culture, and joy, that connects all of us across the spectrum of time—emergent from the past, grounded in the present, and optimistic about a visceral, imaginable, and aspirational future. Old binaries, like our old politicians, have little power on that horizon. As Laurie Anderson and Walter Benjamin and Paul Klee so famously and unambiguously declared through their own respective media, history is an angel being blown backward, into the future. 🏛

This Pepsi-Cola sign (1940), built atop the Pepsi bottling factory in Queens, was designated an individual landmark in 2016. At 50 feet in length, it was the longest electric sign in New York State when constructed. PHOTO: BENJAMIN NORMAN.

MICHAEL KIMMELMAN

THE NEXT FRONTIER:
INTANGIBLE HERITAGE

IN APRIL 1969, two months before police officers raided a gay bar on Christopher Street in Greenwich Village called the Stonewall Inn, New York City's Landmarks Preservation Commission designated the Village a historic district thanks to its row houses and spaghetti entanglement of streets, the serendipity of Colonial-era cattle paths and property lines colliding with the city grid.

With its renovated façade of brickwork and flower boxes from the 1920s, Stonewall occupied a pair of former horse stables and was not particularly distinguished. By 1969, its interior had become a fire hazard. During the 1930s, it was a dive bar and restaurant called Bonnie's Stonewall Inn, which shuttered in 1954. Three years later, the Genovese crime family reopened the bar, retaining the Stonewall sign and name. Gay bars were mostly mob-run back then because of long-standing laws against homosexual behavior in public. Police raids, though frequent, were typically settled with mob payoffs. They rarely turned violent. This time, though, patrons fought back.

The Stonewall raid supercharged the gay rights movement, but the bar itself shuttered soon afterward. The Genoveses sold the property. The spot morphed into a bagel shop. During these years, when no one yet talked about designating Stonewall, the designation of the Village helped forestall proposals to demolish the building. As Andrew Berman, the executive director of the Greenwich Village Society for Historic Preservation, points out, the ear-lier Village designation "made possible what happened half a century later"—namely, Stonewall's own designation in 2015, after gay marriage had become the law of the land. By then, Stonewall had become a pilgrimage site. And a new bar—with the old name, its interior now spruced up for tourists—had moved into the space.

But what exactly was landmarked?

The Landmarks Preservation Commission's designation meant that Stonewall's owners could no longer alter their brickwork or flower boxes without city permission. But the commission regulated nothing to do with the building's use. Nothing today prevents the site from reverting to a bagel shop or becoming a nail salon or a dentist's office. The Landmarks Law does not address function.

That's not an oversight. The law was established not to regulate activi-ties or businesses but to safeguard buildings and other historically significant structures, which is easier said than done. In 2016, for example, the commis-sion designated a popular neon Pepsi-Cola sign in Long Island City from the 1940s, overlooking the East River. The commission had been debating the sign's designation for nearly thirty years. The sign originally stood atop Pep-si's Long Island City bottling plant. Over the decades, its lettering was altered to keep pace with the rising price of a bottle of soda. The sign was swapped out entirely for a new one after a storm damaged it during the 1990s. Then it was moved to the shoreline when the plant was razed during the early 2000s to make way for a park.

So what is designated is a newish sign occupying a location entirely dif-ferent from the original one. You almost need a graduate degree in semiotics to grasp the language of the designation that now specifies the shapes and positioning of the neon letters and the configuration of the sign's supporting structure but doesn't technically prescribe that the sign advertise Pepsi-Cola, because doing so could be interpreted as tipping the scales of city government in favor of one company over another.

I begin with Stonewall and the Pepsi sign because they are not the 42nd

The Stonewall Inn, shown circa 1989. Twenty years earlier, the Stonewall Riots were a significant catalyst for the creation of organizations like the Gay Liberation Front and the Gay Activists Alliance. They were also an inspiration for Pride marches that began in 1970 and continue to this day. PHOTO: EDDIE HAUSNER/THE NEW YORK TIMES/REDUX.

Street library, the Brooklyn Bridge, or Grand Central Terminal. They are not indisputable examples of sublime architecture and engineering. As their tortured designations make plain, they have been designated for other reasons—yet at the same time they are, I suspect, what a wide swath of the general public assumes the law exists to preserve: valued and significant places and things that give the city and its neighborhoods their character, distinction, vitality, social cohesion, and meaning.

At few times in history have so many New Yorkers expressed as much fear around losing what they most love about the city they call home. Crime is low, and the pandemic has subsided. But pessimism is high. New York today faces an unprecedented affordable housing crisis. Covid changed working habits enough to alter the economics of city labor. The income gap has never been wider. Partly as a consequence, new development of almost any sort has come to be viewed as a call to the barricades not only in wealthy, NIMBY enclaves that for years have weaponized preservation—and environmental—legislation to try to maintain zones of exclusivity. This is now also the case in middle-income neighborhoods, and increasingly in vulnerable communities, which fear gentrification because it can lead to displacement. New York has become a very different city than the one that passed the Landmarks Law sixty years ago, when it was possible for working people to find an affordable home, and parents could expect their grown children to find similar homes in the same neighborhood if and when the time came.

What New Yorkers today worry about losing and want to safeguard is not (necessarily) old architecture but what can feel like an increasingly fragile, complex ecosystem of daily life. The threat isn't just to monuments like the old Penn Station but to neighborhood tentpoles like viewsheds, tenement housing, playgrounds, community gardens, and the local Y.

Sometimes these disparate places and neighborhood "landmarks" are loosely grouped together under the phrase "intangible heritage," a squishy term of art. Before New York passed its preservation law, Japan had enshrined its own intangible heritage, which included sites like the Ise Shrine, whose origins date back more than two thousand years. The shrine is ritually dismantled and rebuilt every twenty years, in keeping with Shinto beliefs and practices. *Miyadaiku*—carpenters and artisans to whom the skills needed to reconstruct the temple have been passed down for countless generations—are the keepers of this particular form of intangible heritage, which in Japan can also attach to master calligraphers and theatrical companies. During the 1950s, Japan placed the great Ningyo Johruri Bunraku puppet theater on its national list of Intangible Cultural Property.

Following Japan's example, UNESCO more than two decades ago established global lists of intangible cultural heritage, which the organization broadly describes, in its usual bureaucratese, as "the practices, representations, expressions, knowledge, skills—as well as the instruments, objects, artifacts and cultural spaces associated therewith—that communities, groups and, in some cases, individuals, recognize as part of their cultural heritage."

Translation: intangible heritage need not be a building or a place. It can also include the French gastronomic meal, Moldovan blouse embroidery, and traditional ensembles of xylophone players distinct to southern Mozambique, among myriad manifestations of arts and crafts that nations have nominated for inclusion on UNESCO's lists.

Of course, arts and crafts only begin to describe what a wide swath of New Yorkers regard as local heritage, worth protecting. Cultural mapping is another term of art these days, which more broadly refers to how communities identify key stakeholders and institutions. It's squishy, too. I would guess that, for example, bourgeois Upper West Siders might include a legacy business such as Barney Greengrass, the smoked-fish restaurant, on a cultural map of their district. Many of them might consider it more urgent to safeguard the Sturgeon King than to designate, say, another great Emory Roth–designed apartment building.

Along similar lines, if you were to ask African American residents of Upper Manhattan which building spoke more to their pride of place and identity, the Romanesque revival mansion called the Bailey House from the 1880s—which was built for the circus impresario and designated in 1974—or a derelict, stumpy little house at 857 Riverside Drive, defaced by faux-stone siding, I suspect many would vote for 857 Riverside, because historians have now linked its one-time ownership to an abolitionist who may well have made the house a stop on the Underground Railroad.

But 857 is not designated. Its designation has been thwarted for years by the building's architectural despoliation and a lack of documentation about the Underground Railroad, notwithstanding the fact that the railroad's very existence depended on stealth and a lack of documentation.

In 2022, the Bowne House in Queens was recognized by the United States National Park Service as a member of their National Underground Railroad Network to Freedom program. And the city's Landmarks Preservation Commission has designated 227 Duffield Street in Brooklyn, a nineteenth-century Greek revival row house that, during the Civil War, became home to Harriet and Thomas Truesdell, also abolitionists. As at 857 Riverside, campaigns to designate that building for a long while ran into headwinds about the lack of documentation. But in 2021, after the building's owners announced plans to demolish the row house, and a proposal circulated to replace it with a 13-story mixed-use tower, the rise of Black Lives Matter spurred Mayor Bill de Blasio to intervene and urge commissioners to make the designation. As with Stonewall, politics tipped the scales.

Which raises a question: have commissioners been reading the law too narrowly? It's not a knock on them to ask. They deliberate with remarkable prudence and just caution, but have increasingly come to ask this question themselves.

The original language that established the Landmarks Preservation Commission stressed safeguarding "the buildings and places that represent New York City's cultural, social, economic, political and architectural history." Architecture was just one consideration, in other words. But it became the overriding concern for many reasons: because it was the professional domain of preservationists, who had pushed for the law; because it is far easier to legislate than intangible heritage; and, of course, because the law emerged from outrage over the demolition of a great work of architecture, the old McKim, Mead & White Penn Station. Since then, commissioners have come around to the notion of designating less distinguished historical buildings, including tenements, because of their cultural and social significance.

But the legislation remains a dull instrument for preserving all those other things that "represent New York City's cultural, social, economic, political" history, which, in a different context, Jane Jacobs once defined as the "enormous collection of small elements" that ensure "a lively city"—things like the corner bodega or neighborhood bookshop or community center or farmers market or street fair. The list goes on.

We are getting closer, I think, to what intangible heritage really means, or ought to mean, and why, I suspect, it is the next frontier for preservation in New York. The complications it raises differ from the ones involved in designating, say, mid-century office towers on Park Avenue, or enshrining brutalist, postmodern, and other buildings from the late decades of the last century, which are not universally admired but, with time, have reached the radar screens of concerned architectural advocates. Such buildings pose aesthetic questions. It has become established practice that commissioners consider only aesthetics and history, abstaining from factoring in politics or weighing too heavily the economic consequences of their decisions, because those issues can seem ephemeral, whereas preservation is about the long term.

But the Landmarks Law specifically laid out that one of its purposes was to "strengthen the economy of the city." This discrepancy between the law and how it is practiced often leads to public confusion and distress. When commissioners recently okayed a proposal to build a mixed-use tower on the site of a longtime surface parking lot at the South Street Seaport, opponents of the development claimed that the commissioners had been swayed by developers' promises to include subsidized apartments and money for the struggling South Street Seaport Museum, which the opponents believed should not have been taken into consideration.

But is this quarantining of aesthetics and history even sensible? What is it we are hoping to safeguard? Is it not the lifeblood of the city? And does that not include the ongoing welfare of neighborhoods, which includes their intangible heritage?

Determining what is intangible heritage requires going down a rabbit hole. It means addressing issues now outside the commissioners' purview, issues involving social practices, environmental justice, shifting city demographics, and the economic inequities built into our free-market system.

Should the city preserve, say, its shrinking Flower District? What would that mean, practically speaking? Would it mean specialized tax breaks and subsidies? Like the Garment District to the north, the Flower District is but one of dozens and dozens of clusters that once defined the commercial geography and culture of the city. Before online shopping, these specialized districts emerged from a shared desire among business owners to achieve a kind of critical mass that would help to attract consumers.

Not long ago, the Meatpacking District, whose location depended on the West Side's elevated freight tracks and Titan's comb of industrial piers, was still a cluster of blood-soaked cobblestone streets. Now the old railway viaduct has become the High Line, and the packing plants and warehouses have been converted into Hermès shops and luxury hotels. There used to be a philately district near Park Row and Nassau Street; a millinery district between 35th and 39th Streets during the interwar years; and a fur district where the campus of the Fashion Institute of Technology is now. The Twin Towers replaced an electronics district where, starting in the 1920s, New Yorkers went to buy new parts for their old radios. For years, before the towers were mourned, New Yorkers complained about the giant skyscrapers having erased a human-scaled, working-class neighborhood, turning it into a windswept plaza.

But, practically speaking, what would it have meant for New York to have embalmed a district devoted to record players, Princess telephones, and rabbit-eared, cathode-ray television sets? How differently would Lower Manhattan have evolved? It is one thing to preserve an old building, or even a cluster of storefronts for businesses that once sold turntables for 78s and transistors, another to privilege the outmoded industries these storefronts served in the name of preservation, which runs up against the city's economic interests and mantra of change, not to mention Americans' core belief in individual property rights.

The Meatpacking District in lower Manhattan reflects New York City's industrial landscapes in their evolution from active commercial sites to gentrified residential neighborhoods.
PHOTO: EDMUND VINCENT GILLON/MUSEUM OF THE CITY OF NEW YORK.

Several years ago, the Landmarks Preservation Commission, over the objections of its owner, designated an 11-story building whose base had long been occupied by the Strand Bookstore, one of the last remnants of Book Row, the storied district of used bookshops that defined Fourth Avenue below Union Square in the last century. The Strand's owner vigorously fought the designation, arguing that landmark regulations would saddle her thin-margin business with potentially crippling restrictions and financial burdens. Preservationists countered that the 1902 building, designed by William H. Birkmire, deserved landmark status for its Italianate architecture, which formed part of an ensemble of historic office buildings. The preservationists feared new glassy towers replacing the old office buildings, as was happening at Union Square.

The general public, for its part, no doubt assumed the issue of designation applied to the bookstore, not the building. It was the Strand, after all, not the building by Birkmire, that countless New Yorkers and other book lovers around the world wanted to safeguard, notwithstanding that the store's owner argued that the very act of preservation might doom her business. In the event, the designation has not seemed to interfere with the Strand's fortunes. But neither has it served them.

So then, if the landmarks legislation is not an instrument for that purpose, what might be?

An answer begins with an acknowledgment that we do tip the scales, in all sorts of ways, and we have for years, to favor certain enterprises over others. Since the 1960s, for instance, New York has established special-purpose districts, dozens of them, whose provisions often include preservation goals. A district was created to preserve and strengthen the character of Little Italy in 1977, and another to sustain 125th Street as an arts and business hub with its mix of commercial buildings and historic row houses. A special-purpose district for Clinton, a neighborhood bordering Midtown, was devised in 1974 to shield its residential, mixed-income community from new development. Yet another was established to favor maritime development in Sheepshead Bay in Brooklyn as a means of extending that district's historic character.

How effective have these special-purpose districts been? The legislation carries little, if any, enforcement power. Today most of the neighborhood that comprised Little Italy is a golden memory; stretches of 125th Street have become unrecognizable; Clinton, unaffordable. So the scales were never tipped far—but the precedent was established.

And of course the city has always offered substantial tax breaks to developers and banks to do business in the city, including billions of dollars in tax incentives vainly offered to Amazon to open a headquarters in Long Island City at the very same time the Landmarks Preservation Commission was considering whether to landmark the Strand's building—in essence, offering to subsidize the behemoth competitor of a bespoke and beloved local business.

The question is: Can similar financial advantages be extended to legacy enterprises cherished by their communities?

San Francisco provides them. Certain districts of the city have rules by which chains and franchises must first receive permission before they can move into a neighborhood, as a means of privileging family and home-grown businesses. Blue Bottle Coffee opened its first brick-and-mortar site, a kiosk, in San Francisco's Hayes Valley, and the disincentives there for the chains afforded Blue Bottle a critical boost in its early years, allowing it to grow in the absence of a Peet's or Starbucks. San Franciscans have also approved a ballot initiative establishing the Legacy Business Historic Preservation Fund. In effect, it allows endangered local businesses and storefront nonprofits that have been around for at least twenty years to apply for time-limited grants sufficient to bridge modest gaps between their survival and closure but not so large that the grants are wasted on a doomed and destitute enterprise.

The idea behind the fund is to keep prized, viable, long-standing institutions afloat and in place. New York State has followed San Francisco's lead, creating its own Historic Business Preservation Legacy (HBPL), which has enshrined cherished city businesses like Sahadi's, the Middle Eastern grocer in Brooklyn. The HBPL awards these businesses a medal, but not yet a grant. San Francisco's initiative also started as an honorific, which evolved into a fund. New York State's registry requires a business to have been in operation for at least fifty years in the same municipality. It must "demonstrate a contribution to the municipality's history and/or the identity of the municipality." And it must continue to serve the same industry, meaning a car dealership can't take over the name and storefront of an old soda fountain and then apply for the registry. New York City could establish its own criteria—deciding how many years in business, whether the business can have moved, whether its ownership or name can change.

Would a family-run restaurant like Barney Greengrass be the same, and registry-worthy, if the business were sold to Long John Silver? Would it be right to insist the mob still ran Stonewall? There is no economic or moral reason to resuscitate the fur district.

As the preservationist Michelle Young has described such a potential registry, funds could be granted partly via a public voting process, the rest by a select committee. Perhaps certain city fees could also be waived. We are dealing here with aiding enterprises that the current landmarks legislation was not designed to safeguard.

We have still left unexamined the larger, even squishier but more profound aspects of intangible heritage, or whatever we decide to call it, which will challenge coming generations to think differently. Erica Avrami, a professor of historic preservation at Columbia University, calls this "second-order" thinking.

"We are expecting too much of the existing landmarks law now," she believes. "It is doing a form of design review, looking at places based on visual associations and narratives, whereas communities think if they get something landmarked or districts designated, they can prevent change, gentrification, displacement, which the law has little or nothing to do with. We haven't yet gotten to second-order preservation—thinking of neighborhoods as systems, with distributive effects across the city. Second-order thinking means accounting for the unintended consequences of saving a building, which may include climate change or social justice.

"You can designate a lot of beautiful buildings," Avrami elaborated, "but if they're mostly about white architects designing for white clients, you've centered a particular narrative. What are we saying when we do that?" She points to studies by scholars at the Furman Center showing that New York's historic districts skew toward wealthier, whiter populations. More and younger preservationists today, Avrami says, have come to recognize the built-in bias of their discipline and now have "a strong desire to bust this narrative open"—to tell more stories about more people.

But this will require more than designating buildings like 857 Riverside. That is "representational justice," according to Avrami, meaning just a question of totting up numbers of landmarks, which still doesn't alter who writes the rules or who is advantaged by the designations. She calls these other concerns forms of "procedural" and "distributive" justice. It is a matter of distributive justice, for example, that the Federal Emergency Management Agency will grant extra money to aggrieved homeowners in National Register districts; and that certain energy codes exempt historic districts. As a consequence, designated New York City buildings like Lever House and the Empire State Building don't have to comply with energy codes that other buildings do, implicitly disadvantaging owners whose buildings are not designated. That may be necessary. Is it just?

We are now falling down the rabbit hole. Climbing out is the task ahead. Fortunately, we have a few footholds, which demand flexibility. The zoning resolution that created the Theater Subdistrict some dozen years ago to conserve Times Square and ensure its economic development has managed to preserve that neighborhood's theater life without tying the hands of theater owners by allowing them to transfer air rights within the district. The money raised partly subsidizes discounted tickets and also provides grants to playwrights from underserved city communities. This all occurred because, for once, a strategy of urban planning arose in tandem with preservation, which in New York too rarely happens. As a consequence, the city now protects a use—plays and musicals—and not just buildings that serve the use.

In the future, the city may also wish to think more like Japan, in terms of not only physical permanence but also practice. A farmers market, for

Once the site of an active shipping industry, Valentino Park and Pier in Red Hook, Brooklyn, preserves the memory of Louis J. Valentino, Jr., who demonstrated selfless devotion to fighting fires and saving lives. PHOTO: KARSTEN MORAN.

example, may be a neighborhood staple that a community wishes to preserve, but it comes and goes. The space it occupies is a void. What the community wants to safeguard is not the void, but the market, which changes over time.

Avrami left me with another example of flexible thinking from the late 1980s, when she was a young employee at the New York City Department of Ports and Trade. The Coffey Street Pier in Red Hook had been a tentpole of that Brooklyn neighborhood since the 1600s and by the 1800s had become a bustling center of New York's shipping industry. But by the 1980s, the industry was gone and the Army Corps of Engineers was set to tear down the crumbling pier with its postcard view of the Statue of Liberty. The community was heartbroken. It loved the pier, just not the concrete company next door, another mob-run operation, which had been dumping waste in the water.

Avrami surreptitiously took Polaroids of the dumping from a Coast Guard launch and nudged colleagues at Ports and Trade to do soundings along the shore to prove the waste had altered the water's depth. The concrete company was hit with fines and finally moved. The pier was rebuilt and renamed the Valentino Pier.

As Avrami recalls: "Did it have the original pilings and decking? Of course not. The waterfront had evolved. The original materials were not what community members wanted to save.

"They wanted to save a place where they could walk out over the water, see the Statue of Liberty, and smell the fish and salt air." 🏛

A travel agency ghost sign at West 39th Street and Eighth Avenue, Manhattan. PHOTO: DAMON WINTER.

GHOST SIGNS:
NEW YORK BETWEEN NOSTALGIA AND AMNESIA

1.

DURING THE FIRST MONTHS of the Covid-19 pandemic, when staying home was what united New Yorkers in their solitude, I read a lot of poetry. One of the poems that I found myself coming back to, worrying at it like a sore tooth, savoring it like a slice of layer cake, was "An Urban Convalescence" by James Merrill, the first selection in his 1962 book, *Water Street*.

Personal illness—the clammy, restless state of being sick in the city, with whatever bug is making the rounds—is less the subject than the pretext. Merrill is concerned with a more general, more elusive affliction, a syndrome both chronic and acute. New York itself is the invalid.

The speaker, on the mend from an unspecified ailment, emerges from his house to discover a scene of destruction:

> Out for a walk, after a week in bed,
> I find them tearing up part of my block
> And, chilled through, dazed and lonely, join the dozen
> In meek attitudes, watching a huge crane
> Fumble luxuriously in the filth of years.

The spectacle of wreckage leads him, in the next stanza, to a more general observation: "As usual in New York, everything is torn down / Before you have had time to care for it." These lines balance melancholy with a confession of indifference: what pains him is that he can't or doesn't care. Witness to a moment of loss, he finds himself unable to put his finger on what he and his neighbors are losing. The demolished structure has been forgotten before it's even gone: "Was there a building at all?" he wonders.

With some effort, he summons the vague memory of "a presence," "some five floors high, of shabby stone," which he admits he may be confusing with "another one / In another part of town, or of the world."

This is how the world changes around you: you don't know what you've got until it's gone, and even then you're not so sure. You grasp the presence of something—a structure, a place, a feeling—by reckoning backward from its absence. The process is endless, and also reversible: you can fill in the blank space on the street with whatever comes next. You suspect that will vanish in its turn, condemned before it's even built.

The cycle of building and unbuilding leaves the city dweller in a state of weary, agitated cynicism:

> It is not even as though the new
> Buildings did very much for architecture.
> Suppose they did. The sickness of our time requires
> That these as well be blasted in their prime.
> You would think the simple fact of having lasted
> Threatened our cities like mysterious fires.

"The sickness of our time" is a phrase the poem almost immediately disavows as the kind of slick, summarizing language, "bright but facile," that "enhances, then debases what I feel." The phrase itself is a symptom of what it names: a cold fixation on the present.

The gale of destruction—the "Gospels of ugliness and waste, / Of towering voids, of soiled gusts"—that claimed the anonymous 5-story building down Merrill's street would raze Penn Station a short while later, a catastrophe that galvanized the movement for historic preservation.

I've always associated "An Urban Convalescence," a poem of the early

Interior view of Pennsylvania Station (1910) by architects McKim, Mead & White, photographed by Berenice Abbott, 1936. Its infamous demolition took place from 1963 to 1966. PHOTO: BERENICE ABBOTT, MUSEUM OF THE CITY OF NEW YORK.

1960s, with the old Penn Station, a grand urban edifice that I only knew by its absence, as a symbol of the New York I would never experience and a specter haunting the city I knew.

"An Urban Convalescence" foretells the fate of other American cities, too, whose architectural splendors would be blighted and battered by the growth of the suburbs, the rise of the Sun Belt, riots and rebellions—by actual fires, in many cases. "The sickness of our time" has a way of laying waste to some of our most beautiful structures, abandoning them just as their aesthetic value becomes apparent.

But not all of them. Some things last. Merrill, who lived in Rome before he wrote "An Urban Convalescence" and bought a house in Athens a few years afterward, was exquisitely aware of the way those ancient cities set themselves against the ravages of the future. Among his role models was the Egyptian poet Constantine Cavafy, whose verses about his native Alexandria, written in Greek, treat the ancient and modern incarnations of the city as a single, continuous polity. In Cavafy's lyrics, characters and incidents from the first and second centuries are as immediate, as intimately known, as their early-twentieth-century counterparts. The essential facts of urban life—sex, commerce, politics, gossip—don't change, and the streets and buildings bear witness to their endless ebb and flow. The poet, summoning ghosts, is as familiar with the ancient dead as with his own contemporaries. Or rather, because they occupy the same city, the dead are his contemporaries.

New York is a much younger city than Rome or Athens or Alexandria, a capital of modernity as they are monuments of antiquity, but "the simple fact of having lasted" renders it, like them, both vulnerable and durable. It's accessible to memory and fantasy, even as, in reality, it continues to mutate and evolve. Merrill's poem concludes—the urban convalescence is achieved— when he returns to his desk and finds that "back into my imagination / The city glides, like cities seen from the air." This thought guides him back to earth, descending from a romantic vision of a different city altogether ("that honey-slow descent of the Champs-Elysees") into a more humble, habitable view of urban existence. What tethers him to New York is "the dull need to make some kind of house / Out of the life lived, out of the love spent."

Merrill was not primarily a New York poet. He and his lover, David Jackson, made their homes in Athens, in Key West, and above all in the seaside town of Stonington, Connecticut. "An Urban Convalescence," opening a book whose title specifies the location of the Stonington house, is one of his few New York poems. It's marked less by a sense of place—the buildings and blocks are hazy; the only street mentioned by name is in Paris—than by the centrifugal, migratory rhythm of the poet's consciousness. He drifts from his block (in Greenwich Village? In Murray Hill? He doesn't say, though he lived in both neighborhoods in the years between Rome and Stonington) into taxicabs and airplanes, to secret locations in his own memory.

"The massive volume of the world / Closes again," he muses. It's a clever double entendre, suggesting both the material solidity of the world and its abstract, immaterial existence in the pages of a book. To live in New York is to float between these realms, between the world of things and the world of signs.

And also between the present and what came before, between the amnesiac "sickness of our time" and the contrary malady of nostalgia. The final poem in *Water Street*, "A Tenancy," makes the connection explicit:

> If I am host at last
> It is of little more than my own past.
> May others be at home in it.

These lines suggest an antidote, or at least a salve, for the malady described in the opening pages of the book—the trampling of the past and the unhousing of memory. Literally, which is to say biographically, the movement from "An Urban Convalescence" to "A Tenancy" traces Merrill and Jackson's flight from New York to the serenity of Stonington. But the last lines of the latter poem don't depend on that kind of geographical specificity. They could speak in the voice of the city itself, inviting strangers to make room for themselves in its history.

That's how I read them anyway, in my private anthology, in which every poet is a New York poet because New York is (as Walt Whitman said of America) essentially the greatest poem.

2.

I can't help myself: literary criticism isn't just what I do for a living; it's how I experience the world. New York was the center of my reading life before it was my home, and at this point there really isn't a distinction. It's impossible to find the boundary between the city of books and writers—*Lyle, Lyle,*

Crocodile, Tell Me a Mitzi, Stuart Little, The Catcher in the Rye, James Baldwin, Mary McCarthy, Dawn Powell, Junot Diaz—and the city of my actual experience. What I've lived is assimilated to what I've read, and vice versa.

But literal New York is also a city of texts, of words, of accidental poems, of prosaic verbal prompts that open up new vistas of imagination. For many years, I sat at my desk in the fourth-floor *Times* newsroom, gazing south down the trough of Eighth Avenue at a hulking, yellow-brick pile rearing up against the sky somewhere around 39th Street. It was not a beautiful or significant piece of architecture—at best, the structures crowding that hectic stretch of Manhattan between Port Authority and Penn Station achieve a thick-shouldered solidity that is the poor cousin of grandeur—and I wouldn't necessarily have recognized it from street level. In any case, it meant less to me as a building than as a piece of literature. On gray afternoons, struggling against deadlines, I would stare through my office window and read what was painted on the north exterior wall.

In big, blocky, black sans-serif letters, someone—an anonymous Walt Whitman on a window-washer's platform, a mid-century "wall dog"—had written a poem for my eyes alone, a song of faraway, sun-kissed places. MEXICO MIAMI PUERTO RICO BERMUDA BAHAMAS. Really, it was antique advertising copy, committed to brick for the benefit of a long-gone travel agency specializing in warm-weather vacations. MEDITERRANEAN MIDDLE EAST GREEK ISLAND CRUISES. Those words, unadorned by images or even adjectives, were sufficient to conjure in me the longing for another world.

I imagined a mid-century version of myself, in an office floating above the avenue, shirt cuffs unbuttoned and necktie tight, the air thick with cigarette smoke and typewriter racket, seduced from my drab everyday routine into a dream of paradise. A cruise. A beach. LOS ANGELES. LAS VEGAS. Another island. A different city.

That dreamer was himself a dream, a specter summoned into my shiny, digital, screen-dominated present by the presence of that ghost sign. He wished he was in Miami; for my part, I wanted to travel back to a Manhattan where a spell of tropical escape could be cast by a simple message on the side of a building.

Ghost signs are not uncommon in New York and other cities of its vintage, but encountering them is always surprising, and a little uncanny. Often, you don't notice them at all, but once you do they haunt you, becoming part of the strange, familiar landscape of your days.

I used to drive past one in Brooklyn, at the confluence of Bedford and Flatbush Avenues, urging residents to vote for John Lindsay, the Republican candidate for mayor in 1965. The faded, blue-and-white paint, still legible nearly sixty years later, promises a bright future for New York.

A faded ghost sign in Brooklyn, near Bedford and Flatbush Avenues, recalls the Mayor John V. Lindsay era. PHOTO: KARSTEN MORAN.

Lindsay—a handsome, patrician congressman from the Upper East Side—won that election, which took place the year before I was born. At the time, my grandparents lived about a mile southeast of that sign, in Midwood. They were loyal lower-middle-class Jewish Democrats, so it's likely they voted for Abraham Beame, Lindsay's Democratic opponent. It's also possible that they voted for Lindsay in 1969, when the Republicans dropped him and he won reelection on the Liberal Party line in an especially fractious five-way race. I never had a chance to ask them about that, but I would think of my grandparents every time I drove past the sign on my way to Brooklyn College or Maimonides Hospital or the Kings Plaza mall, trying to measure the distance between their Brooklyn and mine, trying to map time onto geography.

The first New York I knew firsthand was Lindsay's, where I visited my grandparents from whatever academic outpost my parents were living in at the time. My memories are vivid, though I don't entirely trust them; they're memories of memories, mental ghost sightings of handball courts, the Coney Island boardwalk, subway cars blanketed in graffiti, pizza slices and Italian ices, the lengthening shadows of a summer evening on the East 16th Street sidewalk.

My grandparents left New York at the end of the 1970s, having taught in its public schools, broken up fights on its sidewalks and subway platforms, paid taxes and union dues, and otherwise contributed to its civic flourishing. When I moved to Brooklyn in the early 1990s, I encountered many ghosts. This feeling isn't uncommon for new arrivals or generation-skipping returnees, but it always manifests itself in specific, idiosyncratic, private ways. We each decode the signs in our own particular way and summon shades of meaning that speak only to us. And so I would sit in my office on a gray afternoon and daydream of booking a GREEK ISLAND CRUISE. I would drive down Bedford and pull the lever for John Lindsay and fun city. If people wanted directions to my house, I would tell them it was a few blocks south of Ebbets Field, where the Dodgers used to play before Walter O'Malley spirited them away to Los Angeles in 1957.

Ebbets Field, the home of the beloved Brooklyn Dodgers baseball team (1913–1957), was demolished in 1960 after the team moved to Los Angeles. It was replaced in 1962 with high-rise housing, named the Ebbets Field Apartments. PHOTO: MOA ART/OLD NYC PHOTOS.

The ghosts cluster close to home; that's what makes it home. My house, in the shadow of Ebbets Field's shadow, had a basement adorned with vintage textured red vinyl banquettes, a cork ceiling, and a compact wet bar. At some point between the departure of the Dodgers and the end of the Lindsay mayoralty, this low-ceilinged room must have been a blind pig, an off-the-books night spot with space in one corner for a drum riser and a tight little band.

Before that, it had been a doctor's surgery. The block, developed in the

1920s, was known as Medicine Row because of the physicians, associated with Kings County Hospital, who set up their private practices in these stately free-standing brick houses.

The doctors moved away. The basement bacchanalias fell silent. The hospital still stands, hulking above the roofline of the neighborhood like a fortress. The promise of Lindsay's city—the New York in which the Landmark Law was enacted, a New York of hope and heartbreak—was still palpable to me on my daily walks and Saturday drives.

3.

According to Colson Whitehead, "you are a New Yorker when what was there before is more real and solid than what is here now." This condition of temporal and existential displacement may look like a cure for Merrill's "sickness of our time," which erases the old before anyone has time to appreciate it, but really it's a different strain of the same disease. Before long, what is here now will turn into what was there before, and the void of the present will fill up with nostalgic meeting, and you will join the ranks of the ghosts.

In *Netherland*, his novel about life in New York before and after the attacks of September 11, 2001, Joseph O'Neill captures the local dialectic of amnesia and nostalgia by means of an improbable horticultural metaphor. "You might say, if you're the type prone to general observations"—which I am—

> that New York City insists on memory's repetitive mower—on the sort of purposeful postmortem that has the effect, so one is told and forlornly hopes, of cutting the grassy past to manageable proportions. For it keeps growing back, of course.

This image owes something to Andrew Marvell, the great English rhapsode of mowing, and to Walt Whitman, the Brooklyn-born bard of grass and the first self-proclaimed New York poet. More to the point, perhaps, *Netherland* is a novel about cricket, a pastoral pastime very much concerned with the practical and aesthetic demands of lawn care.

Cricket is also among the most popular, fastest-growing participatory sports in New York, embraced by immigrants from South Asia, the Caribbean, and other corners of the former British empire. (From elsewhere, too: O'Neill's narrator, Hans van den Broek, learned to bowl and bat while growing up in The Hague.) New York was also once part of that empire, with its own half-obscured place in the history of cricket. Hans's friend Chuck Ramkissoon, a garrulous, entrepreneurial Brooklynite who came to the city from Trinidad in the 1970s, dreams of reviving and expanding that tradition by building a state-of-the-art complex devoted to the sport at Floyd Bennett Field, the airstrip from which Charles Lindbergh and others made record-breaking flights. In the meantime, the game is played in makeshift pitches, mainly in the outer boroughs, where groups of men gather on weekend afternoons.

Those matches become Hans's primary experience of New York life—the thing that swings him from nostalgia to amnesia, that concentrates his attention on the present even as it propels him back into the turmoil, disappointment, and fleeting happiness of his pre–New York past.

Netherland is a populous novel about loneliness. Hans is a familiar kind of metropolitan literary type—a wanderer, a flaneur, a solitary rambler like Alfred Kazin in *A Walker in the City*, Julius in Teju Cole's *Open City*, and James Merrill in "An Urban Convalescence." His perambulations, mostly behind the wheel of Chuck's Cadillac, take him far from Manhattan, where he works as an analyst for a global investment bank. A Dutchman, linked whether he likes it or not to the first European residents of New York, he finds an accidental tribe among newer arrivals from Africa, Asia, and the Americas.

The novel explores Hans's friendship with Chuck, the fracturing of his marriage, and his relationships with his dying mother and young son in lyrical chronological disorder. The narrative leaps forward and loops back according to the caprices of mood and memory, but at the center—omnipresent though rarely mentioned—is the destruction of the World Trade Center, which carves an emphatic boundary between Before and After.

To echo Merrill, the towers were gone before we had time to care for them. To some of us, they no doubt still seem more solid and more real than what

A view of the World Trade Center shrouded in fog, circa 1975.
PHOTO: ALLAN TANNENBAUM/GETTY IMAGES.

is there now. The last moments of *Netherland*, unspooling a vivid memory of the towers seen from the water at sunset, by Hans and his mother and other passengers on the Staten Island Ferry, affirm this idea even as they accept its tragic limits:

> To speculate about the meaning of such a moment would be a stained, suspect business; but there is, I think, no need to speculate. Factual assertions can be made. I can state that I wasn't the only person who'd seen a pink watery sunset in his time, and I can state that I wasn't the only one of us to make out and accept an extraordinary promise in what we saw—the tall approaching cape, a people risen in light.

4.

It should go without saying that the city is more than its ghosts, that it is built out of substances more obdurate than nostalgia, amnesia, and desire. But my argument, my hunch, is that without those vapors and whispers, it would disappear. They leave their traces in books, poems, and songs, but mostly they exist unseen and unrecorded, in the impressions left on and by the people who stayed long enough to look at something—a sign, a patch of grass, a home—and wonder what was there before.

The physical infrastructure of New York is durable and also fragile, threatened by neglect and weather, by slow erosion and sudden catastrophe. To have lived through any period of the city's history is to have witnessed dramatic alterations of its landscape as well as more subtle transmogrifications. You can be shocked at what has vanished, and equally surprised at what's still there. It's not necessary to leave the city and then come back to be startled in this way. Maybe a change—of neighborhoods, of jobs, of lovers or friends—brought about an alteration of routes. You took a different train, turned down different blocks, looked elsewhere for diversion. And then one day you find yourself in an old familiar spot that isn't familiar anymore. The bookstore is a bank branch. There's a new sign on the bodega. The squat brick building where you taught freshman composition to art students has been torn down and replaced by something shiny and metallic.

Is this promise or tragedy? Decline or renewal? Those are the wrong questions. It's always both, and the progress or regression of New York is always measured in the feelings of the people who live there.

Some of them write those feelings down, but I take their literary efforts to be representative of a deep, democratic sentiment. Or, rather, a constellation of impressions and intuitions, extending forward in time and glancing backward like the lines of a poem. The city is that poem. We are its ghostwriters. 𝍓

The New York City Hall rotunda (1812) has a keystone-cantilevered marble staircase, one of the first of its kind in the United States, designed by John McComb and Joseph-François Mangin. It remains a feat of engineering ingenuity. PHOTO: GERRY O'BRIEN.

GUY NORDENSON AND NAT OPPENHEIMER

ENGINEERING LANDMARKS

AT THE STILL POINT

FOR REM KOOLHAAS, in his aptly named *Delirious New York*, the concept of a landmark is complex. Structures from the Brooklyn Bridge to the Chrysler Tower and Empire State Building endure, though they are increasingly hemmed in by newer upstarts. This churn has always been thus. In *Gotham*, Mike Wallace and Edwin G. Burrows describe how Joseph Pulitzer's 1890 World Building "was a corporate self-proclamation, a brand name shouting itself in iron and stone, a shrewd Barnumesque statement by a man well aware that appearances could constitute reality."[1] The many skyscrapers that followed in nearly a century and a half are quintessential citizens of the skyline that identifies New York. They represent not only the "speech acts" of commerce but also the alchemy of turning iron and stone into abstract reputation and wealth.[2]

This transmutation is both material and spiritual and, as such, arises from the science and the seeming magic of building. As in real magic, subterfuges are best kept hidden. This hidden tradecraft does not appear in many

---

1 Edwin G. Burrows and Mike Wallace, *Gotham: A History of New York City to 1898* (Oxford University Press, 1998), 1052.
2 See "Tall Building as Metaphor," in Guy Nordenson and Terence Riley, *Tall Buildings* (New York: The Museum of Modern Art, 2003).

133

histories. From Wallace and Burrows to Manfredo Tafuri, among many others, the dialectic of appearances varies only from "a structure materializing the concept of laissez-faire . . . [to] an element capable of exercising a formal control over the urban complex as a whole."[3] Some landmark skyscrapers are acknowledged masterworks of architecture; others are sentimental favorites. Whether just a tall building or a fully realized work of architecture, a building's form, spaces, and appearance are what count. Compare the Seagram Building to the Chrysler Building. A case in point, as we will see, is the late World Trade Center, which clearly served as a landmark though never quite accepted as architecture.

Emphasis on appearance also detracts from the effects of time. Landmarks, including buildings, bridges, and parks, all age and weather. They go through periods of neglect or even come close to demolition, only to be recognized as in need of renewal. Restoration subsequently discloses the inner workings of the buildings, as do landmark expansion projects. And apartment buildings and individual residences, some considered landmarks or included in historic districts, are frequently altered in ways that make them accessible for discovery and interpretation.

During this repair and reinvention, structures and building systems can reveal key aspects of our material culture, including lost forms of engineering practice, material uses, and machinery. Over time, those practice landmark alteration and restoration can discover the deep structure that holds the legacies of engineers, builders, and mechanics who have contributed to our cultural heritage alongside architects, artists, and landscape architects. New York would be a different place were it not for engineers like John, Washington, and Emily Roebling; Othmar Ammann; Homer Balcom; Fred Severud; and Leslie Robertson—whose work is only the tip of a material culture that encompasses centuries of craftsmanship and invention.

Hidden landmarks of remarkable structural inventiveness are scattered

3 Manfredo Tafuri, "The Disenchanted Mountain: The Skyscraper and the City," 419, in Giorgio Ciucci, Francesco Dal Co, Mario Manien-Elia, and Manfredo Tafuri, *The American City: From the Civil War to the New Deal* (The MIT Press, 1979).

throughout New York. Severud designed a tensile roof modeled after a bicycle wheel for Madison Square Garden that, if revealed, might display some of the lost glory of McKim, Richardson, and Van Der Bent's Pennsylvania Station. The stacks of the New York Public Library support both books and building. This system—the work of Angus Snead Macdonald—is pervasive in New York, including in the recently expanded Frick Collection.[4]

Rarely does a single landmark building celebrate these achievements. Rather, the elegance of structural components and engineering is more often expressed in the overall evolution of structures inhabiting the skyline or in clusters of buildings that, taken as a whole, define the architecture of a period. As we celebrate the anniversary of the 1965 landmarks legislation, structural work—both very specific elements and more general trends—deserves recognition as well. As we move into the next sixty years of preserving landmark architecture, this structural work is likely to play a larger and larger role as technology moves forward and these systems age and change.

Landmark preservation requires an acknowledgment of this heritage and allows us to recover these hidden lessons of genius and material practices. In fact, in many cases going forward, it is likely to demand that we understand these practices.

NEW YORK STRUCTURE

The paradigmatic New York landmark is the Statue of Liberty (1881–1884).[5] It is hard to imagine that, had it been the target of the attacks of September 11, 2001, it would not have been rebuilt as it is. The decision about rebuilding the World Trade Center site, for better or worse, was not long in coming. As with most lost buildings of New York, the site would become something else. The drawn-out drama of rebuilding the World Trade Center site, as well as the curious effort to make Hudson Yards another Rockefeller Center, point

---

4   Charles H. Baumann, *The Influence of Angus Snead MacDonald and the Snead Bookstack on Library Architecture* (Scarecrow Press, 1972). Oppenheimer has worked on the Snead bookstacks of the New York Public Library, and Nordenson on the alteration of the Snead bookstacks at the Frick Library.
5   See "Tall Building as Metaphor" (note 2).

to the difficulty citizens and leaders have in deciding what to hold on to and what to cast away. Over time, New York's grid alone endures, freeing the city to constantly transform.[6]

Besides its symbolism,[7] the Statue of Liberty plays a quieter role as a paradigm of New York buildings and landmarks. The statue is the composite work of the sculptor Frédéric Auguste Bartholdi, the engineer Gustave Eiffel, and the architect Richard Morris Hunt. Their works are distinct, with Hunt responsible for the masonry base, Eiffel for the innovative steel and iron pylon and branch structure, and Bartholdi for the form's thin copper leaves, whose prefabrication, using the repoussé method—recommended to him by the architect Eugène Viollet-le-Duc—he oversaw in Paris. The whole can be judged both by its total effect and by the creativity of its parts. Eiffel's inventive structure in particular prefigures the engineering and building art that undergirds the public appearance of many of our landmarks.

With notable exceptions, including the World Trade Center Twin Towers, this composite architecture also "liberated" New York architecture from the geometry of the pervasive frame structures that support it. This approach contrasts with Chicago's architectural history, which is known for the formal innovations of Daniel Burnham, John Wellborn Root, Louis Sullivan,

---

6   "From its discovery, Manhattan has been an urban canvas, exposed to a constant bombardment of projections, misrepresentations, transplantations, and grafts. Many 'took,' but even those that were rejected left traces or scars. Through the strategies of the Grid (with its fabulous incremental receptivity), the inexhaustible *Lebensraum* of the synthetic Wild West of the Skyscrapers and the Great Lobotomies (with their invisible interior architectures), the 1672 map becomes in retrospect a more and more accurate prediction: portrait of a paranoiac Venice, archipelago of colossal souvenirs, avatars and simulacrums that testify to all the accumulated 'tourisms'—both literal and mental—of Western culture." In Rem Koolhaas, *Delirious New York* (Montacelli Press, 1978), 245.

7   On September 14, 1976, the Landmarks Preservation Commission designated the Statue of Liberty, its base, and the land it is situated upon as a New York City landmark; see https://s-media.nyc.gov /agencies/lpc/lp/0931.pdf (accessed April 5, 2024). The Statue of Liberty monument, surrounded by the waters of New Jersey, remains within the jurisdiction of New York State; see "Statue of Liberty a Legal New Yorker, Supreme Court Says," *Los Angeles Times*, October 5, 1987, https://www.latimes .com/archives/la-xpm-1987-10-05-mn-22509-story.html (accessed April 5, 2024). However, in 1998, the U.S. Supreme Court ruled that nearby Ellis Island, also federal property, belongs within the territorial jurisdiction of both New York and New Jersey. The Main Building, housing the Ellis Island National Museum of Immigration, is within the boundary of New York State. However, since the island was expanded over many years to its current 27.5 acres, most of the expanded area falls within New Jersey territory.

Assembling the Statue of Liberty in Paris, from *Album de la construction de la Statue de la Liberté*, 1883. The entire structure was reassembled on Bedloe's Island in 1886, after construction of the pedestal was completed. PHOTO: ALBERT FERNIQUE/THE WALLACH DIVISION OF ART, PRINTS AND PHOTOGRAPHS: PHOTOGRAPHY COLLECTION, NEW YORK PUBLIC LIBRARY.

and Dankmar Adler. Their advancements projected steel-frame geometry and reduced façades to relatively light curtains of terra-cotta and broad bay windows. The firms of both Burnham and Root and Adler & Sullivan saw the formal and practical advantages of opening façades to light and air and shaping the "curtain wall" to flow freely about the structure it both hides and reveals. Where the French engineer Eiffel offered a trunk-and-branch structure independent of form, the Chicago engineer William Le Baron Jenney made structure an actor. Upon inventing the space-filling grid of the frame structure for the Home Insurance Building (1885), Jenney developed the distinct style that Colin Rowe called "Chicago frame," which had so much influence on the emerging modernism in Europe.

The translation and retranslation of the "Chicago frame" from Chicago to the Bauhaus and back produced "a formula . . . permitting the simultaneous appearance of both the structural grid and considerable spatial complexity."[8] This new wave passed first through Chicago, where Mies van der Rohe moved from Germany and where the firm Skidmore Owings & Merrill (SOM) was founded. The spatial and sculptural dexterity of the Seagram Building (1954–1958) and the Lever House (1950–1952), diagonally across from each other, affirms Mies's interpretation. And yet an examination of the structural drawings of both shows that they continue the tradition of pragmatic, often hybrid, structures.[9] While SOM Chicago designed tall and long-span buildings with overtly expressed structure, in New York engineers Leslie Robertson and William LeMessurier hid their artful structures of the World Trade Center and Citicorp Center behind the varied shapes and façades of the buildings' architecture. The elegant variation of steel types used in the Twin Towers of Robertson and architect Minoru Yamasaki, applied by Robertson to direct forces through the tower,[10] was unknown before we produced a drawing to visualize it after September 11. The towers' structure

---

8 See "Tall Building as Metaphor" (note 2), 18 and references.
9 Ibid.
10 Guy Nordenson, "Constellations," in *Seven Structural Engineers: The Felix Candela Lectures* (New York: The Museum of Modern Art, 2008).

The Seagram Building (1958), the only New York City work by architect Ludwig Mies van der Rohe, was designated an individual landmark, and its lobby and its Four Seasons Restaurant were named interior landmarks, in 1989. The elegant juxtaposition of void and solid, expressed through the building's glass curtain wall and extruded bronze members, is considered by many the culmination of the International style.
PHOTO: ANDREW GARN.

was a kind of abstract minimalist sculpture in which each square column and plate beam was identical in outside dimensions, with divergence only in the plate thickness and steel type. Similarly, the AT&T "Chippendale" Building of Robertson and architects Philip Johnson and John Burgee incorporates a holistic structural design that, like Eiffel's for the Statue of Liberty, is independent of the form.

Apart from the overall frame of a structure or tower, in New York other structural components have defined entire eras of architecture (many of which are rich in individual landmarks). Most of these components have remained hidden, except to those fortunate enough to work on the bones of a building.

One of these elements is structural clay tile. Numerous examples of the Catalan Guastavino terra-cotta tile arch system can be found throughout the city.[11] Charles McKim, who saw these vaults as carrying both symbolic and tectonic significance, commissioned builder Rafael Guastavino to create many of them.[12] Even more pervasive in the city are the shaped hollow clay tiles used to fireproof both steel and wrought-iron floor beams and create flat arches spanning the spaces between them.[13] The clay tile arch blocks were closely fitted to the shapes of steel and iron "I" beams, while covering them against fire and grasping support off their bottom flanges to anchor the flat arch that supported the floor above. This system is no longer in use and would likely find resistance from both contractors and building department

---

11 Among many other locations, Guastavino terra-cotta tiles can be found at Grand Central Station, the Queensboro Bridge approaches, the Manhattan Municipal Building, the Cathedral of St. John the Divine, and Low Memorial Library at Columbia University.

12 John A. Ochsendorf, *Guastavino Vaulting: The Art of Structural Tile* (Princeton Architectural Press, 2009).

13 "The visible points of superiority, as compared with similar tile of different makes, are the deep dovetail scoring for the better bonding of stucco or plaster, the absence of imperfections and the better general symmetry due to the more accurate machining by this company's unequaled equipment. Equally important qualities not obtainable in other tile are not so apparent to the eye. These consist of finer properties in the raw clay and its more uniform and thorough burning, resulting in greater density and a higher degree of inherent strength. It is to certify these advantages, and to instantly identify the tile possessing them, that the name NATCO is stamped plainly upon the face of each tile." From the NATCO Catalogue, "Fireproof Construction for Houses and Other Buildings at Moderate Cost," 1910, quoted in Wikipedia, "Structural clay tile."

Guastavino tiles line the ceiling of the South Concourse, David N. Dinkins Municipal Building (1913).
PHOTO: ZACK DEZON.

officials. Yet in the context of the climate crisis, its efficiency and the low embodied carbon of the system is prescient. Ironically, the fragile-seeming tiles have endured as one of the most robust floor systems of their time, continuing to this day to work efficiently and with great elegance.

Structural clay tile systems are just one of many ways that late nineteenth- and early twentieth-century engineers and builders minimized cost while building robust structures. Many of New York's tall buildings, from the original RCA Building at Rockefeller Center to the Empire State Building (both engineered by Homer Balcom), rely on infill masonry walls and clay tile fireproofing to stiffen the tall, open steel-frame structures against the wind. The RCA Building, for example, has no positive lateral system of diagonal steel bracing or rigid frames in the narrow east–west direction but relies, perhaps unwittingly, on the composite stiffness of the masonry-infilled steel frames. Over time, following World War II and the modern movement, these hybrid systems providing multiple functions were replaced by more segregated systems of structure, curtain walls, and lightweight interior partitions. A measure of this shift is the decreasing density of buildings from approximately 30 pounds per cubic foot for the Empire State Building to a third of that for the World Trade Center Twin Towers. In some cases, the shift away from masonry infill left structures too flexible and even unstable.[14] This reductive lightness also facilitates the shift to a commodity economy of buildings that are less likely to be valued as landmarks, as was sadly the case with the Twin Towers.

This evolution in the stiffness of structures has often led to unfortunate moments of discovery, such as the cracking finishes in the Gulf and Western Building that were discovered during alteration work in the 1970s. This

14 One of the cascading causes of the window breakage suffered by the John Hancock Tower in Boston was the absence of a positive lateral wind resistance structural steel system in the longitudinal direction. The New York–based structural engineer, accustomed to the practice in New York of omitting either steel braced or moment resisting wind frames and relying on the masonry cladding and interior partitions, did not recognize that the building curtain wall was all glass and provided no stiffness. Curiously, the engineer called on to help fix the problems with Hancock, William LeMessurier, was also collaborating with that same New York engineer on the Citicorp Tower, which also had some mishaps in construction. Fortunately, both buildings went on to be local landmarks.

damage resulted when a more modern flexible structure was combined with the stiffer, more brittle partitions of the past. The partitions worked without issue in stockier, heavier buildings, but were entirely misaligned with the newer frames. Similar issues have arisen more recently within the tall sliver towers rising along Central Park South. The tower sway sickness that befell inhabitants of Gulf and Western was abated by modern tuned-mass and sloshing dampers, but the building's cracking partitions continue to vex.[15]

A more visible element of the New York landmark vernacular is the "cantilever" stone staircase found at the entrances of many important buildings, including City Hall and the Museum of the City of New York. Following a tradition that reaches back to Andrea Palladio in the Renaissance, and even earlier Greek and Syrian examples, these stairs are made of dressed stone steps and landings that hover off one side embedded in a wall. The stairs appear to cantilever off the wall, an impossibility given the poor tension capacity of stone, but in fact the overlap of each step to the one below means the weight and load of people cascades down each step to the bottom.[16] As with the Guastavino vaults and flat-arch tile floors, the modernization of codes and practices and the loss of craft trades have made these durable structures apparently obsolete. In retrospect, given the increased carbon emissions this modernization has provoked, these techniques and crafts could well be brought back into use as "living treasures."[17]

The history of New York structures is for the most part that of an ecology of emergent technologies that rise and wane and are replaced in each

---

15 Tuned-mass dampers (TMDs) were introduced in the 1970s, in part by LeMessurier, to mitigate building sway. They are generally a fraction, less than half a percent, of the mass of the building, and are designed to move opposite to the building's sway in the wind. Sometimes the mass is solid; sometimes it is made of water in connecting tanks that "slosh." These are now very common around the world for tall, thin towers. LeMessurier installed a TMD in both the Hancock Tower in Boston and the Citicorp Center in New York and claimed to have a key to the room in Citicorp, where he would ride the mass in storms.

16 See Guy Nordenson, "SoHo Stair," in *Reading Structures: 39 Projects and Built Works: 1983–2011* (Lars Müller Publishers, 2016).

17 For example, see the discussion of Japanese "Living National Treasures" at https://www.toki.tokyo /blogt/2023/8/9/living-national-treasures-the-link-between-past-present-and-future.

new cycle. That vernacular is not so well known except perhaps by those charged with the restoration and expansion of those individual buildings that are valued enough to remain amid all the change and "delirium." But these hidden constructions represent another kind of landmark in the city.

TIME'S CHURN

Reflecting on "creative destruction" and the city, the New Yorker Marshall Berman wrote, "Even the most beautiful and impressive bourgeois buildings and public works are disposable, capitalized for fast depreciation and planned to be obsolete, closer in their social functions to tents and encampments than to 'Egyptian pyramids, Roman aqueducts, Gothic cathedrals.'"[18] Landmark laws restrict the extent of this churn by maintaining objects and districts of continuity. In the language of ecology, creative destruction can also be framed as part of the cycles that C. S. "Buzz" Holling associated with ecological (as opposed to engineering) resilience and the corresponding adaptive cycle of growth, development, collapse, and renewal.[19] The related concepts of social-ecological adaptive cycles describe cyclical patterns of nature and societies that not only repeat but also evolve in "nested" cycles. Natural systems, from boreal forests to the Serengeti, transform through cycles of growth, destruction, and regeneration that can extend over decades. To arrest those cycles, say with fire prevention in forests, can risk extinctions. Similarly, to fixate on notions of steady state and equilibrium—the idea in engineering resilience of "bouncing back"—misses the nonlinear dynamics of real urban systems.

It is useful in this sense to study the periodic transformations and expansions of museums and performing arts centers in New York. Both of the present authors have served as structural engineers for these projects, including the Guggenheim Museum, the Museum of Modern Art (MoMA), the Metropolitan Museum of Art, and the Metropolitan Opera. MoMA, for example,

18 Marshall Berman, *All That Is Solid Melts into Air: The Experience of Modernity* (Verso, 1983), 99.
19 Stephen R. Carpenter and Garry D. Peterson, "C. S. 'Buzz' Holling, 6 December 1930–16 August 2019," *Nature Sustainability* 2 (2019): 997–998, https://doi.org/10.1038/s41893-019-0425-9.

Construction of the New York City World Trade Center (1973), a complex of seven buildings that included the Twin Towers, then the tallest buildings in the world. The Towers were destroyed as a result of the September 11, 2001, terrorist attack; the five other buildings sustained extensive damage, and the entire complex was razed. PHOTO: MEYER LIEBOWITZ/THE NEW YORK TIMES/REDUX.

has added buildings over time since its start in 1939, beginning with the building designed by Philip L. Goodwin and Edward Durell Stone. Major expansions have occurred in 1980–1984 with César Pelli, in 2001–2004 with Yoshio Taniguchi, and most recently in 2016–2019 with Diller Scofidio + Renfro (DS+R). Buildings and a garden were added by Philip Johnson between 1950 and 1964. With each cycle, the choices to retain or replace reflected the prevailing taste. Taniguchi aptly captured that dialectic by framing the Johnson garden, painstakingly recreated, in his all-around crisp modernism, while restoring the historic sequence of façades along the side of the 53rd Street entrance. DS+R's addition to the west, including the tragic destruction of the American Folk Art Museum (designed by Tod Williams and Billie Tsien), extended this sequence to include the Jean Nouvel tower at the west end. Along the street, one can follow the history from Goodwin-Stone to Nouvel via Johnson, Pelli, Taniguchi, and DS+R.

From the engineers' viewpoint, this history is also embodied in the multiplicity of structures, enclosures, and systems that emerged from an equally eclectic series of actors. While mostly invisible, a compelling story of New York construction, quite like that of the commercial construction of tall buildings noted above, has been incorporated through these cycles. Both the Pelli and Nouvel towers are built in typical residential flat-plate construction, though the Nouvel tower's jagged profile displays a jazzy version of Chicago-style diagonal bracing. The remaining museum sections are a mixture of concrete and steel framing. The Taniguchi expansion includes mostly invisible nuances in both the structure's tatami-inspired geometry and its extreme minimalism in some places, including the carving of spaces through the Pelli tower to accommodate the reconfigured circulation.[20] What is striking, and very New York, is the feeling inside the fully expanded museum of smoothed frictionless space as one progresses through the invisible history of constructions.

In contrast, the multiple expansions of the Metropolitan Museum of

20 Nordenson, *Reading Structures* (note 16).

Art are more clearly manifest as one moves around its labyrinthine interior. One of the museum's charms is the difficulty of finding one's way, proving a challenge to many young explorers. This palimpsest of architectures presents a very different experience from the MoMA's "make it new" smoothness. Yet here, too, the embedded history of construction is little understood or documented. Morrison Heckscher's excellent history of the sequence of buildings, from those of Calvert Vaux to those of Kevin Roche, shows how each generation of expansion wraps around and both buries and loads the last.[21] Depending on the architect, the corresponding constructions may have some historical significance. The records are limited. In one instance in the 1960s, the lack of understanding and documentation of the Guastavino vaults installed at Charles McKim's direction in the courtyard and gallery spaces of the northern Wing H (1904–1913) resulted in their demolition. They were replaced by a steel and concrete floor for the expanded Egyptian exhibits. As has often happened in New York, a combination of lost craft knowledge and misplaced or nonexistent documentation has led to the demolition of these hidden cultural treasures.[22] At the Metropolitan Museum of Art in particular, given its age and position at the edge of Central Park, a rich material culture and history is subsumed in the walls and floors. These—including the underground and back-of-house hidden mysteries, from water tunnels to vaulted foundations—could warrant a follow-up to Heckscher's history.[23]

The Guggenheim Museum, designed by Frank Lloyd Wright and completed in 1959, is an obvious landmark in many ways, including, in our opinion, structurally. Apart from the more conventional northeast portion of the building (where the stairs and elevators are located), the majority of the

---

21 Morrison H. Heckscher, "The Metropolitan Museum of Art: An Architectural History," *The Metropolitan Museum of Art Bulletin* 53, no. 1 (Summer 1995).

22 Jonathan C. Ellowitz, "Structure and History of Guastavino Vaulting at the Metropolitan Museum of Art" (master's thesis in civil and environmental engineering, MIT, 2014).

23 Nordenson and Oppenheimer are collaborating with NADAAA on the design of the new Ancient Near East and Cypriot galleries at the Metropolitan Museum of Art, which include the alteration of the original south exterior wall of the Richard Morris Hunt Jr. Wing D, which was subsumed into the later McKim Mead & White Wing J, with later alterations by Kevin Roche.

The Guggenheim Museum (1959), designed by Frank Lloyd Wright, posed a complex engineering problem during its restoration in 2005–2008. The solution by Robert Silman Associates required advanced computer modeling combined with daily monitoring of the building's movements. PHOTO: LIBRARY OF CONGRESS.

structure consists of nine cast-in-place concrete radial "web walls" (visible within the galleries), the continuously rising ramp slab (cast-in-place concrete as well), and the iconic façade spiral, which was constructed in concrete using the gunite method (fluid concrete sprayed onto mesh reinforcement, a method more often used to build swimming pool shells or sculpture).

The precise performance of the Guggenheim's façade—both the portions hung from the web walls and those simultaneously bracing the web walls—has not always been evident. While there is a clear structural load path throughout and, by observation, the structure is rigid and laterally capable, in 2005–2008, a structural team, led by Robert Silman, was asked to determine the cause of persistent cracks in the façade concrete that have vexed the museum from the outset.[24] The analysis and fix provide a potent example of using modern analysis tools to assess, and then restore, historic structures. The critical feature of this approach is harmonizing modern digital design programs with archaic structures to ensure that one does not incorrectly ascribe modern properties and behavioral assumptions to brittle elements from an earlier time.

At the time of Silman's analysis, large-scale digital scanning was still relatively early in its use in buildings but had finally become available beyond academic domains. Given the importance and scope of the building, the team leveraged this new technology to scan the entire building into an unimaginable digital cloud of data, which was then converted into a three-dimensional geometric image. They uploaded that image into structural modeling software and analyzed it as a solid concrete structure. This process took months to complete (months alone simply to clean up the data and "mesh" the elements in the model); it would take considerably less time today, as the technology has advanced rapidly in the twenty-plus years since this analysis took place.

Over the long period of modeling, the building was simultaneously monitored under all external conditions on a day-by-day basis, with the eventual intent of calibrating in situ movements with the computer model. Finally, simultaneously with both of these efforts, the team opened physical probes on the façade that unlocked the key to the ultimate design solution: discontinuities in the reinforcing at the circular façade. These discontinuities would not have been visible to any sort of scanning (even today), because the break in the reinforcing was obscured behind other steel elements.

---

24 "Bob" Silman was regarded as the preeminent structural engineer for the preservation of landmarks in New York. He oversaw the repairs to Frank Lloyd Wright's Fallingwater with great skill and inventiveness, as well as Carnegie Hall and the Morgan Library, among many other key landmarks. He and Les Robertson both saw themselves as truly "civic" engineers and contributed greatly to the civility of civil engineering in New York.

By combining each of these steps, the team learned the cause of the cracking and then, most importantly, designed a fix that could be verified with confidence based on the calibration of the digital model with actual behavior in the field. Any one of these approaches might have yielded a supposition or recommendation. Together, model, monitoring, and testing ensured that the fix (in this case, laminating the entire non-historic inside face of the façade with carbon fiber to add tensile strength) aligned with the original intent of the structure. Quietly, hidden behind the finishes, this trifecta returned the structure to its original intent. The churn in this case was more of a technological sort within a unique form.

The Guggenheim, in both its original form and its repair, is a unique example of New York's churn, but another set of structures within New York possesses specific characteristics that allow them to respond to churn in a very specific manner: the city's grand old theaters. New York contains a number of these designated landmarks, which deserve the designation they've been given. Structurally, whether designated or not, they deserve attention and thoughtfulness as the urban fabric changes and the use of these spaces evolves. Although the most famous venues—Carnegie Hall, Radio City Music Hall, the Apollo—will never lose their audience and usefulness, nor their landmark status, many similar spaces are often in danger of demolition because they cannot house contemporary shows, obstruct larger and taller development, or simply are not owned by entities that can afford to maintain them.

The majority of these buildings share two key characteristics that make them uniquely suited for wholesale relocation: they are relatively light (most of their volume is air), and they are contained with a continuous solid masonry shell (darkness being key to their use). The outcome of moving a theater is the retention and restoration of its interior, which is usually the historic fabric of most value in a new and often more economically viable location.

Twenty-five years ago, the Empire Theatre was famously rolled west on 42nd Street to make room for new, contiguous development; more recently, the Palace Theatre on 47th Street was lifted 30 feet above its original foundation to make room for lucrative retail space at the ground level of a new museum complex. In both cases, it is quite likely that, without the renovators' ability to lift or move these theaters, they would have been lost forever. More ambitiously, Zankel Hall was excavated below Carnegie Hall in the early 2000s, while Carnegie Hall remained open and operational above.

Lighthouses are often rolled back from the eroding edge of a cliff, or a small private residence is lifted to avoid future storms, but very few structures in the urban landscape are lifted or moved. When the DS+R plan at MoMA was first announced, a small group of designers and builders proposed rolling the American Folk Art Museum to another site. Ultimately, the size and density of the building made that impossible. But theaters are, in many ways, uniquely suited for this version of churn and rebirth.

HOME

The development of residential buildings in New York, especially multifamily ones, is rich in social history, not all of it pretty. The structure of apartment buildings played a minor role in that history. The early nineteenth century was the era of the wood and masonry bearing wall tenement building. By the late nineteenth century, the so-called prewar apartment buildings of Emery Roth, H. J. Hardenbergh, and Rosario Candela were steel frames clad in stone with infill masonry that acts, often unwittingly, as the lateral system that supports the building from collapsing under wind loads. These are robust landmarks in both presence and substance, supported by the fact that many of Candela's buildings, among others, exist to this day, including 720 Park Avenue, 1 Sutton Place South, 960 Fifth Avenue, and 1 Gracie Square.

While his portfolio has too many great examples to suggest the designating of "Candelas," several consistent structural themes within the buildings are critical to the history of New York residential buildings. His structures harnessed and accelerated the use of the steel skeleton to support all gravity loads. Not until 1968 did New York formally require designs of structures under 100 feet tall to support wind loads (and not until 1992 were buildings required to withstand a seismic event), and, in many cases, buildings over

100 feet tall were assumed to be capable of supporting wind loads based on their significant masonry façades, although that was rarely, if ever, a quantitative determination. The reality is that most buildings, other than ground-breaking towers, were not designed to support lateral wind loads prior to 1968 and were assumed to be "shielded" by their neighbors or otherwise buttressed within the city's dense grid.

The absence of any lateral requirements freed the architect to place columns anywhere in the floor plan, which is the hidden magic of these classic apartment buildings. This freedom is a clear precursor to modern cast-in-place concrete residential buildings, where lateral loads are often supported by large concrete cores (at the stairs and elevators) or portions of the façade (often in rear façades, not visible to street view), and columns are free to roam.

Starting in the 1920s, the use of lightweight "cinder" concrete slabs and the aforementioned terra-cotta tile systems added to the unique aspects of these structures. Cinder concrete substituted economical industrial cinders for sand aggregate and was reinforced with continuous wires draped from beam to beam. The concrete was very low strength—approximately a third of conventional cast-in-place concrete at the time—and essentially performed as a solid walking surface, with the wires behaving as short-span suspension bridges from steel beam to steel beam (thus the term "draped mesh slabs" was often used). Like their terra-cotta counterparts, these slabs survive to this day as a generally robust and well-regarded floor system, although renovations and wear and tear are, in some cases, beginning to signal the slow end of the cinder slab's usefulness.

Because the slab was not considered a key element in the overall structure, bays could be dropped to the bottom of the beams in bathrooms (allowing for ornate stone finishes flush with the wood and carpet finishes throughout the balance of the apartments) or raised (to allow for a higher ceiling in the apartment below).

Taken together, the offset columns, the unreinforced masonry façades, and the discontinuous, low-capacity slabs represent a textbook assembly of modern seismic fatal flaws, with the masonry considered too brittle (non-ductile) and the floor slabs unable to carry forces to the exterior walls. However, these structures do persevere and do legitimately rely on their neighbors for support, meaning that New York, over time, is likely to face the conundrum of maintaining these buildings in perpetuity, side by side, or retrofitting those structures that are left alone on a block, with new structures potentially rising to the left and right.

In the postwar era, the construction of apartments was gradually cheapened, and few buildings of the 1950s and 1960s are as notable. Exceptions include the Manhattan House of Gordon Bunshaft and the Imperial House of SOM and Emery Roth & Sons. But even these have required maintenance of the thin-glazed brick façades that replaced the more robust (and costly) masonry façades of the prewar era. Later decades saw the emergence of the flat-plate concrete apartment buildings engineered by Robert Rosenwasser, Jacob Grossman, and Irwin Cantor. These include a cluster of tall, thin buildings around Carnegie Hall, all three engineered by Grossman; many others by him and Rosenwasser, including César Pelli's Museum Tower; and the original Trump Tower on Fifth Avenue, engineered by Cantor. The industrial engineering marvel of this flat-plate construction, like earlier New York–based inventions, combines a thin slab or "plate" of reinforced concrete without beams with concrete walls around the buildings' cores. This affords low floor-to-floor heights, a relatively random arrangement of columns to suit the apartment layouts (the link to prewar styles), and, most importantly, a rapid construction that allows one to two floors to be built every week. Plate construction became the "Broadway Boogie Woogie" of concrete.

PRESERVATION, CONSERVATION, CODES

Structures do not last forever. Rules of thumb used to guide engineers through the renovation of wood and masonry townhouse construction evolve every twenty years or so as these buildings age and their characteristic strengths start to fail. Structures once thought significantly robust—and their cost, at the time of construction, supported that claim—are now often seen as brittle and potentially dangerous during a seismic event by modern engineering standards. Height-to-width ratios once thought unimaginable are now the norm, and the sway of these newer buildings runs the risk of threatening their older neighbors all around them if they are not properly designed and managed.

Structure evolves like anything else, and New York is generally the better for it. But what to do with the structures that define an era and, more importantly, continue to perform well, even if they do not meet the modern standards set for new construction? While adaptive reuse of a historic masonry building is one of the best approaches we can take to limit embodied carbon within a project, many solid masonry buildings need significant work to meet equally important energy standards. Even within the preservation community, the debate is constant and ongoing about whether to preserve a structure "back to its original" or to ensure that the renovation work gives the building another hundred years of life and updates its structure to meet modern good practice (and further debate occurs about what represents "good practice" in historic masonry structures).

Modern model codes,[25] including the relatively recently introduced International Existing Building Code (IEBC), take a somewhat prosaic approach to this question. If one does more than a certain percentage of work within the building, and/or removes more than a certain percentage of structural strength, one must upgrade the building to modern code requirements. The IEBC does make an exception for formally designated buildings, recognizing that forcing an engineer to retrofit a historic landmark may result in more damage to the historic fabric than the potential extreme event you are retrofitting against. Nonetheless, this exception begs the question inherent within this essay: what constitutes a structural landmark that might be hidden within an unregistered historic building?

---

25 Nordenson initiated and led the development of the New York Earthquake Regulations from 1984 to their enactment into Local Law 17/1995, signed by Mayor Rudy Giuliani on February 21, 1995; see Robert Olshansky, "Making a Difference: Stories of Successful Seismic Safety Advocates," *Earthquake Spectra* (Earthquake Engineering Institute) (May 2005), https://doi.org/10.1193/1.1902953.

More importantly, over the years we have seen the evolution of codes and the appropriate ongoing consideration of seismic detailing and performance of unreinforced masonry (URM) during a seismic event. The recent past has suggested that unreinforced masonry bearing walls are the absolute poorest performer during seismic events. This is based on sound reasoning, since URM walls are stiff (so they absorb more of the force of the event than a more flexible system), brittle, and discontinuous, with catastrophic shear failure being a significant concern.

Yet, over the past few years, new studies have emerged indicating that these walls perform even worse when supported by new steel frames that have been inserted delicately (and sometimes not) into historic structures. These new frames presumably buttress a fragile masonry wall but instead generate incompatibilities that often do more harm than good. Couple that with studies that indicate that masonry walls will often fail and crack to a degree but, within that movement, will develop hinges and joints that dissipate seismic energy and ultimately weather the event.

Presently there is no conclusion to this conundrum. As an engineer tasked with preservation or conservation or adaptive reuse, do you follow the basic rules of the IEBC and simply retrofit if told, or do you treat the structure as a landmark of its own, asking the structure what role it should and can play in its new life?

CONCLUSION

One does not often find as clear a connection between structure and architecture in New York as one does in Chicago. Many New York landmarks designated for their architecture have included a significant number of notable structural features. Though some of these features might well qualify as landmarks in their own right, the hidden history of New York structures and construction is frequently lost to demolition.

Many structural designs and systems have influenced the architecture of great swaths of the city and advanced the practice in ways that were taken for granted in their time. Too often characterized as "archaic" and dismissed as being from another time, many of these systems prove more robust and capable than assumed.

Making structures resilient often means constructing them in a durable, fortress-like manner—holding back the seas, organizing with some vision of the future worker, and building with new materials that are seen as impervious to the elements. Yet to this day, the most resilient buildings within New York—including the designated landmarks (which often have had a single use and have been beautifully maintained throughout the years)—are apartment buildings like those of Candela and Roth and the masonry and heavy timber factories that populate the city's long and winding waterfront.

We recognize that the cast-iron buildings of SoHo, the old concrete and masonry warehouses and printing plants of Hudson Square, and the few remaining sheds along the waterfront are beloved vestiges of earlier times both in spirit and in their material grit and resolve. That spirit, echoing these grittier, less ritzy landmarks, returns as ghostly and evocative silhouettes in the structural art installation *Day's End*, by David Hammons (2014–2021). 🏛

Day's End by artist David Hammons (G. Nordenson, engineer), in Hudson River Park, is a "ghost monument" that precisely follows the outline of the demolished 1975 work of the same name by artist Gordon Matta-Clark, carved into an abandoned pier shed once located at Pier 52 and transformed into a sculpture celebrating water and light. PHOTO: SIMBARASHE CHA.

With its outstanding neon airplane sign, the Air Line Diner on Astoria Boulevard is visible from Grand Central Parkway, Queens, to travelers en route to LaGuardia Airport. PHOTO: ALAMY.

ANDREW DOLKART

WHAT ELSE TO CONSIDER:
THE NEXT SIXTY YEARS

IN 2025, the New York City Landmarks Preservation Commission turns sixty. As is customary at most diamond anniversaries, we have much to celebrate. In 1965, when the city council passed and Mayor Robert Wagner signed the bill that created the Landmarks Preservation Commission, no one imagined how far-reaching this law would be and how much of an impact the Landmarks Preservation Commission would have on the character of many city neighborhoods. In its six decades of active responsibility for the preservation of New York's architecturally, historically, and culturally significant sites, the commission has, as of 2024, designated almost 38,000 properties, including 1,464 individual landmarks, buildings in 157 large and small historic districts, 123 interior landmarks, and 12 scenic landmarks.[1] Combined, these designations make up about 4 percent of the city's building lots.[2] This is an enormous responsibility for one of the city's smallest agencies. Perhaps the most significant aspect of the anniversary celebration is that the Landmarks Preservation Commission survives at all, as it has withstood intense

---

1   The home page of the Landmarks Preservation Commission's website has the most up-to-date statistics on designations; see https://www.nyc.gov/site/lpc/about/about-lpc.page.

2   Regarding percentages of designated structures, the total number of taxable properties in New York City in 2022 was 1,134,390, per *The City of New York Annual Report of the New York City Real Property Tax*, Fiscal Year 2022; see https://www.nyc.gov/assets/finance/downloads/pdf/reports /reports-property-tax/nyc_property_fy22.pdf (accessed April 3, 2024).

opposition from powerful real estate interests, editorial opposition from local media, and neglect from politicians.

But before we break out the champagne, we should note that the commission's future remains uncertain; political support has been lacking, and the traditional opponents of designation, such as the Real Estate Board of New York, joined by new groups such as Open New York, seek to limit the agency's prerogatives. Over the decades, the commission has been falsely accused of responsibility for many of the city's ills. Designation has allegedly lowered property values by restricting development, and raised property values through gentrification; and discriminated on economic and racial lines, although some of the most vocal advocates for preservation in their neighborhoods are Black and Hispanic New Yorkers. It has prohibited change and created frozen-in-time "museum districts," although many historic districts, such as SoHo, Greenwich Village, Jackson Heights, and Fort Greene, are some of the liveliest neighborhoods in the city—among other baseless claims. Yet such allegations continue. In recent years, the designation of landmarks has been blamed for the city's crisis of affordable housing, even though 96 percent of lots in New York City are unregulated by the Landmarks Preservation Commission. And who would want to live in a city where historic buildings that give character to the neighborhoods have been swept away by new development? For it is the multiplicity of historic neighborhoods, of varying scales, ages, and building types and the juxtaposition of old and new buildings, that makes New York such a dynamic city and attracts residents and tourists to its neighborhoods. Indeed, the city's diverse residents, from all boroughs, have been vocal advocates for preserving buildings and neighborhoods and the character that makes each urban neighborhood unique.

The Historic Districts Council, a local preservation advocacy organization (I am on its board), works with more than five hundred neighborhood partners located throughout the five boroughs.[3] Remember that the roots of

---

3   See the Historic Districts Council website at https://hdc.org/ (accessed August 4, 2024).

preservation in New York City are with progressive advocates who sought to preserve buildings and the character of neighborhoods in order to provide livable communities for all New Yorkers. As architect Robert A. M. Stern has so eloquently stated, "The city's historic fabric is what makes New York relevant, livable, and distinct, creating value, stability, and a sense of time and place. The fact that historic preservation reinforces these qualities, that it is a vitalizing force in neighborhoods, is insufficiently recognized."[4]

After sixty years and so many designations, one might conclude that the Landmarks Preservation Commission has nothing left to designate. But this is far from true, as is evident in the number of, and diversity of communities whose residents are advocating for historic district designation and the many significant individual buildings that still lack protection. One of the beauties of New York's Landmark Law is that it does not prescribe exactly what is and what is not a landmark. Sites must be thirty years old and of architectural, historical, or cultural significance, and historic districts must have a "sense of place." Within these broad parameters, every generation can interpret and reinterpret what is worthy of designation.

In its early years, the commission focused on the designation of very old buildings and buildings of aesthetic or architectural significance. Surprisingly, despite the early emphasis on age and aesthetics, sixty years after the creation of the commission, major works in these categories, all across the city, still have not been designated. Here is just one outstanding example in each borough: the 1763 Dutch Colonial–style Old New Dorp Moravian Church on Staten Island; the 1857 Gustav Schwab House, a rare example of an Italian villa in the Bronx, located on what is now the campus of Bronx Community College; Ralph Adams Cram's Russell Sage Memorial Church (now the First Presbyterian Church of Far Rockaway, 1908–1910), which contains the largest stained-glass window ever designed by Tiffany Studios, and is set in a landscape by Olmsted Brothers, in Far Rockaway, Queens;

---

4   Robert A. M. Stern, "Introduction," in *Saving Place: 50 Years of New York City Landmarks*, edited by Donald Albrecht and Andrew S. Dolkart with Seri Worden (New York: Museum of the City of New York and Monacelli Press, 2015), 17.

Buildings of historic significance still lack landmark designation, including the Dutch Colonial–style original New Dorp Moravian Church (1756), founded by one of New York City's oldest Protestant denominations. The former church now houses cemetery offices and is the second-oldest church building in Staten Island. PHOTO: KARSTEN MORAN.

Cass Gilbert's astonishing, monumental reinforced-concrete Brooklyn Army Supply Terminal (1918–1919) in Sunset Park, now a city-owned manufacturing and warehousing center; and the Equitable Life Assurance Society's rental office for the King Model Houses (later Strivers' Row) at 252 West 138th Street in Harlem, an elegant little Venetian Gothic building designed by Jardine, Kent & Jardine in 1895 that later housed the offices of the Coachmen's Union League Society, an organization of

Black chauffeurs, and is now a church that is stranded just outside of two historic districts.

These sites stand out to me as a historian of the architecture and development of New York City. After studying architectural history and preservation in graduate school, I began my professional career working at the Landmarks Preservation Commission in the late 1970s and early 1980s. I was involved with surveys of historic structures in Brooklyn and the Bronx and wrote designation reports for historic districts and individual buildings, almost all of which were designated for their architectural value, reflecting early ideas of what was worthy of the commission's attention. Since then, I have consulted on preservation issues throughout the city, have been a professor of historic preservation at Columbia University since 2003, and have written extensively about New York City's architecture and development. I have also explored almost every neighborhood in the city.

As I have become more familiar with the city and its neighborhoods, my ideas concerning what is worthy of preservation and designation have evolved beyond the recognition of important architecture. I now understand the value of preserving New York City's vernacular buildings—its typical tenements, apartment buildings, industrial lofts, and mid-century modern office towers. In addition, I, along with much of the preservation community, have come to understand that preservation is about people and that recognizing sites of cultural significance, whether or not they are architecturally valuable, is essential. This concern for cultural sites that reflect the diversity of the city's population over time is crucial to comprehending the complexities of New York's history and also invites people of myriad backgrounds into the preservation fold.

While architecture has been maintained as an important value for designation, the criteria for preservation have expanded over the decades. This is evident in the Landmark Preservation Commission's equity framework for designations launched in 2021, "prioritizing designations that represent New York City's diversity and designations in areas less represented by landmarks."[5]

---

5   "LPC Launches Equity Framework," New York City Landmarks Preservation Commission, press release, January 19, 2021.

Despite the equity framework and recent designations relating to African American, Latino, and LGBTQ histories, designations that focus on cultural issues continue to be difficult for the commission. For decades, the commission was hesitant to designate cultural sites, ostensibly because of concerns about how they should be regulated, although it seems obvious that each site would be regulated to maintain or restore the features from the time of its cultural importance.

Some of the most rancorous efforts of recent years to designate landmarks relate to efforts to save cultural sites. St. Brigid's Roman Catholic Church on Avenue B and East 8th Street, a Gothic Revival–style church that is an early work by prolific Catholic-church architect Patrick Keely, is strongly associated with the history of Irish famine immigrants. Shockingly, no landmarks specifically commemorate this key nineteenth-century immigrant group in New York City. Despite vigorous community efforts, the commission refused to designate this church when it was in danger of demolition, claiming that it had been altered, but ignoring the fact that the cultural link to the Irish history of New York and not the building's aesthetics is what is paramount with this site. Only after a court order and an anonymous gift of $20 million was the church restored and reopened in 2013. Similarly, the commission has continuously rejected the designation of a group of beachside bungalows located in Far Rockaway, rare survivors of working-class summer communities that once existed throughout the Rockaways. And like the Irish, the Chinese community is woefully underrepresented in designations, with only one recent designation—a small veterans' memorial located on a traffic island in Chinatown.[6]

With its focus on architecture, the Landmarks Preservation Commission has not found it easy to assess cultural sites that are devoid of aesthetic interest. This situation began to change with the 2019 designation of African American author and activist James Baldwin's house at 137 West 71st Street, a nineteenth-century row house that had been altered in 1961, before Baldwin

---

6   The 1962 Kimlau War Memorial was designed by Chinese American architect Poy Gum Lee.

purchased the property, into a banal white brick box. But the commission still does not know how to deal with sites of cultural significance that have been altered. The Walt Whitman House at 99 Ryerson Street in Brooklyn exemplifies this issue. Both the poetry community, represented by the Walt Whitman Initiative, and the LGBT community, through the NYC LGBT Historic Sites Project (I am a cofounder and codirector of this group), have been advocating for the designation of what is the only survivor of the many houses in New York City where Walt Whitman lived. True, the house has been substantially altered—a story has been added, and the wood siding is covered in vinyl—yet this is where Whitman lived when *Leaves of Grass* was published.[7] In rejecting many requests for a public hearing on possible designation, the commission has continually argued that the building has been extensively altered and that Walt Whitman would not recognize it if he walked down the street. This may be literally true, but the connection to Whitman is still palpable at this address and the building's survival should be ensured by designation, permitting the commission to eventually guide its restoration to a condition more closely resembling that which Whitman knew. Many buildings that were designated years ago for their aesthetic importance have had serious alterations but, thanks to designation, have been carefully restored.

Many buildings and sites, as well as potential historic districts located across the city, should be considered for landmark designation. As I travel around New York and visit its neighborhoods, I am struck by the fact that a number of important building types are underrepresented by designations. Here are two of these types as representative of the wide variety of sites that should be designated as landmarks.

Since the 1980s, in a movement often referred to as "commercial archaeology," roadside buildings have been subject to preservation efforts across the country, except in New York, which has no individually designated gas stations, diners (the Empire Diner on Tenth Avenue is located within the

---

7   NYC LGBT Historic Sites Project, Walt Whitman entry, written by project codirector Jay Shockley (2017), https://www.nyclgbtsites.org/site/walt-whitman-residence/.

These beachside bungalows in Far Rockaway, Queens, on the Atlantic Ocean, are uncommon survivors of once-numerous early twentieth-century working-class summer communities. PHOTO: DEENA SUH.

Chelsea Historic District Extension), or motels; only a few early garages are designated as landmarks, largely for their architectural significance.[8] For me, the most obvious example of a roadside building that should be a designated landmark is the streamlined aluminum Air Line Diner (now Jackson Hole Diner; Mountain View Diner Co., 1952) in East Elmhurst, a neighborhood with no designated landmarks. This diner, clearly visible to everyone traveling to or from LaGuardia Airport on the Grand Central Parkway, retains a superb neon airplane sign.

We New Yorkers like to think of our city as a mass transit center. However, while the subways and buses are crucial to the economic success of New York (and many subway stations are designated landmarks), the automobile has had an enormous impact on the physical fabric of New York, and this fact should be recognized. In one of its most innovative actions, the Landmarks Preservation Commission designated the street pattern of Dutch New Amsterdam, and it has also designated Frederick Law Olmsted and Calvert Vaux's nineteenth-century Ocean and Eastern Parkways in Brooklyn as scenic landmarks. But what about the impact that automobile roads have had on the city? The Bronx River Parkway, among the world's earliest limited-access automobile parkways, is best known in Westchester County, but it begins in the Bronx where several brick and stone bridges designed by Charles W. Stoughton in 1918 are extant at Gun Hill Road, and where portions of the original road alignment may also survive. The Westchester portion of this parkway is listed on the National Register of Historic Places, but no effort has been made to recognize the importance of this pioneering parkway in New York City. Largely under the direction of Robert Moses, New York expanded parkway construction. The Grand Central Parkway was built in conjunction with the 1939 World's Fair in Flushing Meadows Park. Although this parkway has been significantly enlarged, at least one of the original rest areas, a small home-like stone structure, is extant near LaGuardia Airport. And at the Belt Parkway, constructed in the late 1930s along the southern edge of Brook-

---

8 This topic was codified by Chester H. Liebs in *Main Street to Miracle Mile: American Roadside Architect* (Boston: New York Graphic Society, 1985).

lyn and Queens with both vehicular lanes and extensive recreational facilities, an Art Deco service station and the diminutive Plum Beach information pavilion are extant and await recognition in areas also devoid of landmarks.

Interest has increased in the designation of mid-century modern buildings, a field in which New York City pioneered. The commission has designated most of the world-famous examples, such as the Seagram Building, Lever House, and the Guggenheim Museum, and has begun to venture into less well-known buildings. But surprisingly, one important aspect of modern design has been completely ignored by the commission—public schools. The commission has designated dozens of nineteenth- and early-twentieth-century school buildings, but the only designated modern schools are a small number located within the boundaries of historic districts. After World War II, New York City funded major public-school construction throughout the city. New schools were built in outlying areas that were undergoing rapid development, and in older neighborhoods school construction often coincided with major urban renewal projects. In Manhattan, this pattern was especially true in Harlem, on the Lower East Side, and on the Upper West Side. New school design broke from the historical styles of prewar buildings and also reflected progressive educational theories and new ideas of what children needed in education and how schools could contribute to their communities.

In 2013, I led a historic preservation studio at Columbia that undertook a survey and analysis of all of the postwar public schools in Manhattan. This survey uncovered an extraordinary range of architecturally significant schools that reflect the commitment the city made to provide a quality educational environment for all students.[9] Although the survey was limited to Manhattan, it made clear that significant schools exist throughout the city. The Board of Education designed some schools in-house and also commissioned designs from architects from across the United States; many of these buildings incorporate important works of art. As urban renewal was transforming the East River waterfront on the Lower East Side in 1953, the Board of Educa-

---

9 "Mid-Century Modern Schools: Preserving Post-War Schools in New York," Columbia University Graduate School of Architecture, Planning and Preservation, studio report (2013).

tion commissioned a new building on Avenue D and East 12th Street from Harrison & Abramovitz, just after Wallace Harrison had completed his stint coordinating the designs for the United Nations headquarters. The brick, concrete, and glass PS 34, with its *piloti* and bands of windows, is an outstanding example of the influence of Le Corbusier, whom Harrison knew from design work at the U.N. An important feature of almost all of the postwar schools is the incorporation of art into the design. For this school, Harrison commissioned an exterior fence, *Fables of La Fontaine*, designed by Mary Callery (whose sculpture is hung above the proscenium of the Metropolitan Opera House), and an auditorium with murals by Bruce Gregory that reflect the influence of the Fernand Léger murals in the General Assembly chamber at the United Nations, where Gregory had served as an assistant.[10] This auditorium should be an interior landmark.

East Harlem experienced major renewal in the 1950s, especially as the Puerto Rican population in the neighborhood expanded. In 1956, innovative modern school architects Perkins & Will of Chicago received the commission for PS 7 on Lexington Avenue and East 120th Street, designing one of New York's finest low-scale International-style buildings, with a double-E plan consisting of rectilinear pavilions clad in glass with blue spandrels. Elsewhere in the city are excellent examples of the work of Edward Durrell Stone (PS 199, 1960–1963, West End Avenue and West 70th Street in the Lincoln Square Urban Renewal area); Kelly & Gruzen (JHS 22, 1955–1957, Houston and Columbia Streets on the Lower East Side); and the pioneering African American architect from Los Angeles, Paul Williams (PS 154, 1960–1964, 250 West 127th Street in Harlem).

Progressive educational philosophy in the immediate postwar years called for the expansion of vocational education, and New York City responded with the construction of several enormous vocational high schools, combining academic facilities with workshops for specialized vocational training. A particularly notable example is the former William E. Grady Vocational

---

10 Michele Cohen, *Public Art for Public Schools* (New York: Monacelli Press, 2009), 122.

In 1956, Bruce Gregory completed two colorful, biomorphic murals for the newly constructed PS 34 on East 12th Street in Manhattan. PHOTO: KARSTEN MORAN.

High School, 25 Brighton 4th Road, designed in 1956 by the local firm of Katz, Waisman, Blumenkranz, Stein, Weber, a firm that was especially unusual in the 1950s because two of its name partners were women. The building is located in Brighton Beach, a neighborhood with no landmarks. It has a straightforward white brick, glass, and metal panel classroom wing with a monumental brick, stone, and concrete auditorium and gymnasium pavilion with a large relief sculpture by Costantino Nivola and a concrete entrance ramp leading to doorways crowned by a spectacular mosaic mural, *Science and the Humanities*, by Ben Shahn. The question remains, why does this building, as well as the others discussed here, remain unprotected?

The takeaway from this brief essay is that preservationists still have a lot of work to do. The Landmarks Preservation Commission has plenty to keep it busy for many years to come. It is imperative that the preservation community and the commission reach out to the media and to local politicians, educating them about the value of preservation, so that a wide spectrum of voices can respond to unfounded criticisms of designation. Preservation proponents must advocate with owners, communities, and the commission for the designation and protection of the outstanding examples of New York City's architectural, historical, and cultural heritage, so that our neighborhoods continue to be diverse places with important historic and contemporary buildings and remain vibrant places to live and work. 🏛

Jamaica Bay, an 18,000-acre wetland estuary, is surrounded by the Rockaway Peninsula to the south, Brooklyn to the west, and Queens to the east. Largely undeveloped, it is almost equal in size to Manhattan. PHOTO: TONY CENICOLA/THE NEW YORK TIMES/REDUX.

LISA SWITKIN

LIVING LANDMARKS:
TOWARD AN ECOLOGICAL WORLDVIEW

THE NEW YORK CITY LANDMARKS LAW gives the Landmarks Preservation Commission the authority to designate and protect two types of public spaces: scenic landmarks and historic districts. Currently, New York City has twelve scenic landmarks: Central Park, Prospect Park, Riverside Park, Grand Army Plaza, Bryant Park, Morningside Park, Fort Tryon Park, Ocean Parkway, Eastern Parkway, Verdi Square, the Coney Island Riegelmann Boardwalk, and the Old Croton Aqueduct Walk. In addition to scenic landmarks—many of which were designed by Frederick Law Olmsted—the commission has also designated 157 historic districts, with the majority located in Manhattan and Brooklyn. Notably, less than 15 percent of the city's historic districts are located in the Bronx, Queens, and Staten Island, and those boroughs have no scenic landmarks, primarily because the oldest developments are concentrated in Brooklyn and Manhattan. Manhattan is the geographical and demographic center of the city with the greatest density, while Brooklyn is the most populous borough. In 2021, the Landmarks Preservation Commission launched an "equity framework" to address this disparity and better represent the city's true diversity.

As we examine the last sixty years of historic preservation, I would argue that these two categories of public space, while useful in the past, no longer fully capture the value, significance, and diversity of the public realm as we know and use it today. Nor do they reflect what we strive for it to be tomorrow. Research has shown that quality urban public spaces "support mental and physical health, serve critical green infrastructure functions, contribute to economic development, act as links in transportation networks, host cultural and social activities, and help give communities a sense of place." Therefore, in addition to broadening the range of sites and stories, we also need to expand the categories themselves to better reflect the evolving nature and use of our public spaces.

The public realm, which encompasses these outdoor spaces, is integral to how most New Yorkers discover and experience the city. It is where we relax, unwind, and recharge. It is where we meet our neighbors, come together, celebrate, and protest. It is where we commune and connect with nature, and are inspired, enriched, and uplifted. Moreover, landscapes and public spaces are expected to do more today than ever before. After the events of 2020, we have a growing appreciation of open spaces as being essential to our physical and mental well-being and serving as more than just scenery. Imagine the impact if the Landmarks Law were able to recognize landscape as more active, social, performative, alive, and biodiverse. This shift would embody a more ecological worldview, connecting these living landmarks to their broader communities and living systems and significantly altering how we perceive and interact with our environment.

Today, even as an effort is made to increase the diversity of these spaces in terms of location, type, aesthetics, and use, we have no obvious way to acknowledge and safeguard them. I argue that the varied types of spaces that directly impact our daily lives, such as streets and more programmed active landscapes, as well as those that serve a greater ecological purpose, have social, cultural, and historical significance. Expanding the recognition and protection of these spaces to reflect the needs of communities today is essential to ensure that the idea of historic preservation within the Landmarks Law remains relevant and forward-thinking. We must find ways to broaden the criteria for landmark preservation to recognize the essential role that outdoor sites and public spaces play in fostering environmental and social resiliency, in addition to their cultural and historical significance. The preservation of these spaces and their benefits are especially urgent and imperative in today's world, where we must adapt to climate change and increase access and equity with speed and care.

AN EXPLORATION OF THE PUBLIC REALM
Public Realm as Essential Infrastructure

The public realm is generally defined as publicly owned places and spaces that are free of charge and accessible to everyone. It includes streets, squares, plazas, sidewalks, trails, parks, waterfronts, and conservation areas. However, the definition of the public realm varies among cities, regions, and cultures and is often nuanced to reflect the values of a particular place with its unique history and traditions. Despite many people considering the public realm as backdrop and scenery, it is central to our lives. It is literally how we move through and about the city, and where we spend much of our time outside of home and work. In New York City, the public realm is defined as public spaces, including roadways, curbs, sidewalks, plazas, parks, and green spaces.

John King, the urban design critic for the *San Francisco Chronicle*, wrote that, of the many profound changes experienced by cities in 2020, the most meaningful might be the "realization of the importance of public space in all its forms, as well as heightened expectations of what such spaces should provide." During the pandemic, the appreciation of public spaces as essential infrastructure was especially pronounced in New York City and other dense urban areas, where shared spaces were the only means of respite. As noted by the Trust for Public Land, the pandemic revealed to New Yorkers that "parks are not just a nicety—they are a necessity." This sentiment has only grown since then, with an increased focus on improving access and the equitable distribution of quality public spaces. In 2023, in an executive order that appointed New York City's first chief public realm officer, the New York City Office of the Mayor recognized public space "as a vital piece of the City's infrastructure that affects the quality of life for all New Yorkers."[1]

New Leadership

In recent years, two new types of city leadership positions have emerged in cities across the world: the chief resilience officer (CRO) and the chief public realm officer. The CRO position was first established in New York City in 2016 to prepare the city for the challenges of climate change and to create a more resilient, equitable, and vibrant city. More recently, in 2023, the New York City chief public realm officer was established to serve as a central point of contact, lead interagency coordination, and drive reform and innovation to improve user experience and create extraordinary public spaces to aid the city's economic recovery. The Alliance for Public Space Leadership marked the chief public realm officer's one-year anniversary by recognizing several accomplishments, including a permanent outdoor dining program for the city, the expansion of Fifth Avenue's holiday Open Street, the creation of Gotham Park under the Brooklyn Bridge, and the completion of a new phase of the Broadway Vision plan in the Flatiron District.

The newly created positions require a deep understanding of the character of the city and how it works and having a vision for its future. These new roles are designed to provide leadership, break down silos in city government, and build partnerships, with open space and the environment at their core. The creation of new leadership positions represents a first step in recognizing the importance of landscape and giving it agency, value, resources, and visibility. Furthermore, the positions provide a framework for a unified and holistic approach to climate adaptation and public space that aligns with the city's equity and climate resiliency goals. Although still experimental and

---

1   Quality of life is highlighted in *The Global Street Design Guide*, a report that sets a new global baseline for designing urban streets prepared by the Global Designing Cities Initiative (GDCI), founded in 2014; see "Streets Shape People," in *The Global Street Design Guide* (Global Designing Cities Initiative, NACTO, and Island Press, October 13, 2016), chap. 1: "Defining Streets," section 1.6, pp. 12–13.

evolving, these positions signify a new era of prioritizing the environment and public space in New York City. With resilience and the public realm finally at the forefront, or at least at the table, it is time to take advantage of these opportunities.

Reimagining Public Streets

New York City streets and street life are the most iconic and defining feature of our public realm, serving as both our backyards and front yards. Streets make up more than 25 percent of the city's land area and provide a platform for social gatherings and interaction, cultural and artistic expression, shopping, and dining. Cities worldwide, propelled by the pandemic and aligned with environmental targets, are reimagining their streets to prioritize people over cars. Recent transformations and reclaiming of streets—such as the revisioning of the Champs-Élysées in Paris, Michigan Avenue in Chicago, Regent Street in London, Avinguda Diagonal in Barcelona, and Pitt Street Mall in Sydney—are evidence of this shift in thinking.

The concept of walkable, pedestrian-centric streets is not new, but it has been gaining momentum in New York. Recently, we have witnessed the transformation of Times Square, the conversion of vehicular roadbeds into new pedestrian plazas in the historic Meatpacking District, and the development of shared streets like Berry Street in North Brooklyn. Other proposals, such as the Future of Fifth, a park-to-park vision from Bryant Park to Central Park, aim to create a vibrant promenade for pedestrians by expanding sidewalks, improving lighting, and increasing greening and seating.

However, refashioning streets is often avoided and contested owing to challenging constraints related to existing conditions and underground utilities, varied ownership and stakeholders, and multiple agencies dictating their design, operations, and maintenance. In response, initiatives such as Streetscapes for Wellness and Streets Ahead are also contributing to the conversation about the role of streets in the city's future. Streetscapes for Wellness aims to change the city's streetscapes through the lens of public health and social and environmental justice, while the Urban Design Forum's Streets

Ahead program envisions a more vibrant and equitable streetscape through the lenses of commerce, culture, climate, care, and continuity.[2]

The historical and cultural significance of streets is also worth noting. As stated by Annah MacKenzie, "Across many cultures and times—since the beginning of civilization, in fact—the street has held vast social, commercial, and political significance as a powerful symbol of the public realm." Indigenous trails, which form the foundation of modern streets, roads, and highways, were conceived as both trails *and* places, and served as conduits of trade and communication and places of cultural interaction. They were designed to work in harmony with their natural and cultural context, following the high ground between watercourses or hills and ridges, and recognizing the land's natural features and flows. Furthermore, indigenous trails were imbued with cosmological significance that was incorporated into rituals, folklore, and mythology over generations.[3]

The Landmarks Law has no specific category for streets, although some— such as Ocean Parkway, Riverside Drive, Eastern Parkway, and the Coney Island Boardwalk—are included in historic districts or designated as scenic landmarks. If we recognize and design streets as places and acknowledge the varied and complex needs of all those who use them, we can create more vibrant communities, encourage sustainable transportation, stimulate local economic opportunities, and increase the urban tree canopy—all of which contribute to improving the quality of life for New Yorkers.

2 "Designing New York: Streetscapes for Wellness" is a publication of case studies released in 2022 to showcase ideas and inspire opportunities for New York City streets. It is a collaboration of the New York City Public Design Commission, The Fine Arts Federation of New York, the New York Chapter of the American Society of Landscape Architects, the New York City Department of City Planning's Urban Design Office, and various other contributors; see nyc.gov/site/designcommission /review/design-guidelines/streetscapes.page (accessed April 8, 2024).

"Streets Ahead" was a year-long effort hosted by the Urban Design Forum from 2021 to 2022 to advance ideas and proposals to envision a more vibrant, equitable streetscape; see urbandesignforum .org/initiative/streets-ahead/ (accessed April 2, 2024).

3 "Today, while it is seldom possible to follow an old Indian path in its entirety, several travelers have attempted to reconstruct them from early maps, travel guides and journals, warrantee surveys, archeological reconnaissance, word of mouth, and field work"; "Native American Trails and Places," Library of Congress Research Guides, guides.loc.gov/native-american-spaces/published-sources /trails (accessed March 29, 2024).

Built on a historic, elevated rail line on the West Side of Manhattan, the original High Line was a continuous, 1.45-mile-long greenway. The Spur (2019) is an extension of the High Line, and the Moynihan Connector (2023) extends east from the Spur to Moynihan Train Hall. The entire High Line has more than 7 million visitors annually. PHOTO: TIMOTHY SCHENCK.

Infrastructure Reuse and Highway Removals

Projects that transform underutilized and neglected infrastructure, including abandoned railways and highways and postindustrial riverfronts and waterways, into new public spaces are becoming increasingly popular and are significantly impacting our built environment. Over the past three decades, New York City has reclaimed its waterfronts, with examples such as Hudson River Park and the East River Waterfront Esplanade in Manhattan; Brooklyn Bridge Park, Domino Park, and Bush Terminal Park in Brooklyn; Gantry Plaza State Park and Hunter's Point South Park in Queens; Concrete Plant Park in the Bronx; and more recently a proposal to revitalize Staten Island's North Shore.

Additionally, the High Line in New York, transforming a 1.45-mile elevated railway into a signature public park, is one of the most recognized examples of infrastructure reuse. The project was completed in three phases, with the first section opening in 2009 and the final section opening in 2019. The High Line has become a model for innovative design, infrastructure reuse, and economic growth, inspiring similar projects around the world—among others, the QueensWay and Bronx River Greenway in New York, The 606 in Chicago, The Underline in Miami, the Bentway in Toronto, and the Waterloo Greenway in Austin. Over the past twenty-five years, Friends of the High Line (FHL) has evolved as an organization with a focus on advocacy for design and construction, as well as maintenance and operations of the park. Recently, FHL has reemphasized its commitment to the community. In 2016, FHL formed the High Line Network to support citizens in finding creative ways to bring green space to their neighborhoods. This peer-to-peer organization brings together more than sixty infrastructure reuse projects to share resources and ideas, learn from each other, and advance the equity movement.

As infrastructure is being reimagined, acknowledgment of the damaging impact highways have had on American cities is growing. Many highway projects in the postwar period divided Black and other minority neighborhoods, increased car dependence, and separated communities from their

The sculpture *Old Tree*, by Pamela Rosenkranz, was commissioned for the Plinth on the High Line at the Spur. Among its many programs, the High Line works with emerging and world-renowned artists to produce new commissioned work for temporary installations. PHOTO: TIMOTHY SCHENCK.

waterfronts. Today, cities across the United States are converting highways into smaller, walkable boulevards, such as the Rochester Inner Loop; covering them with parks, such as the Presidio Tunnel Tops in San Francisco and Klyde Warren Park in Dallas; or removing highways altogether and replacing them with multimodal, at-grade boulevards, as with the transformation of Seattle's central waterfront. In New York, the future of the Brooklyn-Queens Expressway (BQE) has sparked an important debate "regarding the role of the BQE (and more broadly, highways throughout the city)."[4] This conversation has centered on whether to rebuild and expand portions of the highway or to look at alternative community-led plans.

---

4   Beia Spiller and Suzanne Russo, "A Tale of Two Highway Plans," Resources.org, January 17, 2024.

All these projects—reimagined streets, infrastructure reuse projects, and the removal or conversion of railways and highways into new public spaces—are contributing to a new layer of the public realm relevant to the Landmarks Law. They broaden our understanding of the public realm and present opportunities to consider its complicated significance in the city.

AN EVOLVING UNDERSTANDING OF LANDSCAPE

Cultural Landscapes

Cultural landscapes are defined as combined works of nature and humankind. According to The Cultural Landscape Foundation, they are places that provide a sense of identity and belonging, map our relationship with the land over time, and are a crucial part of our national heritage and everyday lives. The UNESCO World Heritage Committee classifies cultural landscapes into three categories: a landscape intentionally designed and created by humans, an organically evolved landscape, and an associative cultural landscape. UNESCO explains that certain cultural landscape sites reflect specific techniques of land use that guarantee and sustain biological diversity, while others embody an exceptional spiritual relationship of people with nature.

The Landmarks Preservation Commission does not have a specific category for cultural landscapes, although one could argue that some cultural landscapes have been designated as historic districts or scenic landmarks, in particular Governor's Island, Ellis Island, and Central Park. The term "scenic" may limit our understanding of these spaces, because it implies something aesthetic, passively enjoyed, and visually pleasing but not necessarily impactful. To fully appreciate cultural landscapes, we need to view them as part of their broader communities and living systems. This approach would recognize how public spaces impact, enliven, and create community cohesion, promote diversity, celebrate culture, and enhance identity.

As of 2022, more than one-third of New York City residents were foreign-born. The "Parks for All New Yorkers: Immigrants, Culture, and NYC Parks" report from 2008 shed light on the importance of how park preferences vary depending on cultural backgrounds. It also highlighted how New York City

Parks has taken steps to address the demand for soccer and cricket fields, offer a greater diversity of foods available in parks, and provide translated signage. In 2014, New York City Parks launched a Framework for an Equitable Future to increase the accessibility and quality of parks throughout the five boroughs. In 2019, the Urban Institute released a report emphasizing the need to direct investments to communities in greatest need to achieve park equity. In 2021, New Yorkers for Parks introduced a "Five Point Plan for Park Equity" platform to increase investment in parks, create a comprehensive parks and open space plan, build more parks in under-resourced communities, reform the citywide procurement process, and empower communities. More needs to be done.

One idea is to recognize more active neighborhood and community-focused public spaces as cultural landscapes deserving of designation. This action would require us to include park use as an important factor in evaluating cultural significance. As part of this effort, we could identify existing culturally significant spaces and suggest new ones that are defined not only by their physical features but also by how they are used and by how they contribute to a sense of belonging for the communities they serve.

Some examples of such spaces include Marcus Garvey Park in Harlem, which has a rich history of activism and culture. In 1835, local residents successfully fought against the city council's plans to extend Fifth Avenue and preserved the area as a public park.[5] The park's renowned outdoor amphitheater hosted the Harlem Cultural Festival in the summer of 1969, which came to be known as "Black Woodstock." Today, significant arts and cultural programming led by the Marcus Garvey Park Alliance, alongside park uses such as swimming, playgrounds, barbecues, and basketball courts, make the park "central to the life of Harlem," serving "as a meeting place for neighbors, a front yard and play area for schoolchildren, and a holy place for members of local churches."[6]

---

5   "In 1835, the Common Council, a predecessor to today's City Council, considered razing the hilly area to accommodate extending Fifth Avenue north of Central Park, but local citizens successfully petitioned to preserve the space as a public park. The land was allotted for public use in 1836 and Mount Morris Park opened to the public in 1840"; New York City Department of Parks and Recreation, nycgovparks.org/parks/marcus-garvey-park/history (accessed April 2, 2024).

6   "Marcus Garvey Park," Harlem One Stop, https://www.harlemonestop.com/organization/25/marcus-garvey-park# (accessed April 8, 2024).

Another public space worth considering for protection is Van Cortlandt Park, located in the Bronx. The park is home to the country's first public golf course (the Van Cortlandt Golf Course, 1895), the oldest house in the Bronx (the Van Cortlandt Mansion, 1748), and the borough's largest freshwater lake (the man-made Van Cortlandt Lake, circa 1690s). Its history is steeped in advocacy for open spaces, beginning in 1888 when the City of New York acquired 4,000 acres of parkland in the Bronx, spearheaded by the city's first open space advocacy organization, the New York Parks Association.[7] In 2021, a portion of the park was consecrated as the Enslaved African Burial Ground with a liberation ceremony, "remembering and honoring the enslaved Africans who indirectly made Van Cortlandt Park what it is today."[8] Today, the park is a hub for community and diversity with popular uses such as playing fields, hiking trails, a nationally renowned cross-country trail, fishing, and horseback riding. Other notable parks worth consideration include Seward Park in the Lower East Side, home to the first permanent, municipally built playground in the nation, and Spring Creek Park in Canarsie, home to New York City's first cricket pitch, which opened in 2003.

A Landscape Approach to the City
Another approach is to create a network of connected public spaces to increase ecological value and impact. As landscape ecologist Richard T. T. Forman has observed, larger patches of green spaces, with corridors between them, lead to higher biodiversity and a healthier environment. Significant health benefits can follow from a "landscape approach" to the city that links green spaces through park districts and connective corridors, including large-scale

---

7   "On December 12, 1888, the City of New York took title to a massive 4,000 acres of parkland in the Bronx, due to the work of the city's first open space advocacy organization, the New York Parks Association. This unprecedented acquisition led to the formation of Bronx, Claremont, Crotona, St. Mary's, Van Cortlandt, and Pelham Bay Parks, as well as Crotona, Mosholu, and Bronx-Pelham Parkways"; "Van Cortlandt Park," New York City Department of Parks and Recreation, nycgovparks.org/parks /VanCortlandtPark/history (accessed April 8, 2024). For a closer examination of the borough that gave us hip-hop and Supreme Court Justice Sonia Sotomayor, see Ian Frazier, "Paradise Bronx," *The New Yorker*, July 15, 2024.
8   Brendan O'Sullivan, "Enslaved African Burial Ground Finally Consecrated," *The Riverdale Press*, June 20, 2021, riverdalepress.com/stories/enslaved-african-burial-ground-finally-consecrated,74939 (accessed April 8, 2024).

ecological landscapes and conservation areas, and comprehensive resiliency projects that connect our city's shorelines.

One idea to consider is the creation of park districts for New York City, similar to historic districts in concept, which would encompass a series of connected open spaces. Park districts in Ohio and Illinois have been created to protect natural areas, preserve open space, and offer educational and recreational opportunities. Illinois is unique in that its park districts are governed by locally elected citizens who have power over the quality and quantity of park and recreation services. Building on the recommendation of the 2020 Building Congress to enact a citywide Public Space Master Plan, park districts in New York could create a unified network, linking existing parks with intentionally designated green corridors. This approach would also work to increase our urban tree canopy, expanding on initiatives such as Million Trees NYC and the New York Restoration Project. One potential corridor could be Fifth Avenue from 124th Street to West 4th Street, linking significant public spaces, including Marcus Garvey Park, Central Park, Bryant Park, Madison Square Park, Union Square, and Washington Square Park. Another example could be a green corridor from Highland Park to Forest Park, connecting significant green spaces from Brooklyn to Queens. If park districts were created in New York City, with the added criteria of enhancing ecological value and function, it could lead to numerous benefits for the city and its inhabitants, as well as our plants and wildlife.

Another strategy is to protect existing large-scale ecological landscapes, natural preserves, and conservation zones and enhance and connect them wherever possible. Examples of landscapes with high ecological value include Jamaica Bay in Brooklyn and Queens, and the Staten Island Greenbelt. Jamaica Bay is over 26 square miles and has been recognized by the U.S. Fish and Wildlife Service as a highly productive coastal habitat deserving of preservation and restoration. Established in 1972 as part of the U.S. Department of the Interior, National Park Service Gateway Recreation Area, it is also the first urban national park. As the largest wetland

Located on the site of a former landfill, Freshkills Park, Staten Island (2008), when completed circa 2036, at 2,200 acres will be the largest park developed in New York City in more than one hundred years. Plans for this enormous park include playgrounds, athletic fields, kayak launches, horseback riding trails, and large-scale art installations.
PHOTO: JADE DOSKOW.

in New York City and one of the country's largest urban wildlife refuges, Jamaica Bay plays a significant role in the ecology of the city. The Staten Island Greenbelt is a 2,800-acre continuous public parkland system of natural and recreational amenities, including New York City's largest remaining forest preserve and a series of "forever-wild" sites. The New York City Parks' Forever Wild Program serves as a precedent for recognizing the importance of preserving the most ecologically valuable lands in the five boroughs.[9]

A less evident example is the 2,200-acre Freshkills Park in Staten Island, which has been transformed and naturalized from a landfill into a public park over the past twenty years.[10] The park could be characterized as an infrastructure reuse project, but it has also become a platform for environmental research, including afforestation, habitat restoration, wildlife biology, soil productivity, water quality, alternate energy generation, and even new attitudes toward park usage. Owing to its scale, Freshkills Park has the potential to make a significant difference in increasing habitat and biodiversity and helping the city adapt to climate change. In 2012, architecture critic Michael Kimmelman noted in *The New York Times* that Freshkills Park "absorbed a critical part of the storm surge" during Hurricane Sandy and buffered neighboring communities from its effects.

Lastly, it is imperative to consider the multiple resiliency projects and waterfront parks that are being developed along New York City's coastline as one integrated coastal protection system and as a public amenity deserving of protection. Several resiliency projects are in various stages of design and construction, with the aim of adapting the city to the challenges of cli-

---

9   "The Forever Wild Program is an initiative of NYC Parks to protect and preserve the most ecologically valuable lands within the five boroughs. The program includes over 12,400 acres of natural areas across 135 parks"; New York City Department of Parks and Recreation, nycgovparks .org/greening/nature-preserves (accessed April 10, 2024).
10 "Freshkills Park will be the largest park developed in New York City in over a century, built on what was once the world's largest landfill. It is being built out in phases, with several projects already open to the public including Schmul Park (2012), Owl Hollow Soccer Fields (2013), The New Springville Greenway (2015), and North Park Phase 1 (2023)." For more information, visit the Freshkills Park Alliance website, freshkillspark.org/the-park/the-park-plan (accessed April 8, 2024).

mate change, providing waterfront access, and protecting our most vulnerable communities. Examples of these projects include Living Breakwaters in Staten Island, the Battery Park City Resilience Projects, the FiDi and Seaport Climate Resiliency Plan, and the East Coast Resiliency Project.[11] Other measures at various scales—such as the earthen berm and increased topography at Brooklyn Bridge Park, the tidal wetlands at Hunter's Point South in Queens, and the development of varied and resilient edges, including tidal pools, ledges, and a salt marsh at Gansevoort Peninsula in Hudson River Park—all contribute to reducing flood risk due to coastal storms and sea level rise. Additionally, they create community amenities and waterfront destinations in the city. While these projects individually increase resiliency and reduce risk, it is crucial to consider the gaps between them and to safeguard them as one unified and linked system.

These sites underscore the importance of "soft" nature-based solutions[12] to create a more resilient New York, moving from the sole use of seawalls,

---

11 "Living Breakwaters is a coastal green infrastructure project designed to reduce erosion and storm damage, improve ecosystem health, and enhance people's experience of the Staten Island shoreline. It it is being implemented by the Governor's Office of Storm Recovery and is funded by HUD through the Community Development Block Grant—Disaster Recovery (CDBG-DR) and New York State. Construction began in 2021 and is scheduled for completion in the Fall of 2024"; for more information, visit hcr.ny.gov/living-breakwaters-project-home (accessed April 10, 2024).

"The Battery Park City Authority is advancing coastal protection projects to adapt to new climate conditions. Design started in 2018, and construction of the barrier systems will begin in 2022"; for more information on the Battery Park City Resilience Projects, visit bpca.ny.gov/nature-and-sustainability/resiliency/ and nyc.gov/site/lmcr/progress/battery-park-city-resilience-projects.page (accessed April 10, 2024).

"The Financial District and Seaport Climate Resiliency Plan is a two-year public planning process launched in 2019 by the New York City Economic Development Corporation and Mayor's Office of Climate and Environmental Justice. It aims to protect the Financial District and Seaport neighborhoods from the impacts of climate change"; for more information, visit fidiseaportclimate.nyc/ (accessed April 8, 2024).

"The East Side Coastal Resiliency Project is aimed at reducing flood risk due to coastal storms and sea level rise on Manhattan's East Side from East 25th Street to Montgomery Street, funded by the City of New York and the federal government. Construction began in Fall 2020 and will continue through 2026"; for more information, visit nyc.gov/site/escr/index.page (accessed April 10, 2024).

12 On December 11, 2023, the U.S. Department of the Interior announced new actions in support of nature-based solutions, which use or mimic natural features or processes to improve biodiversity, strengthen resilience for disaster and hazard-risk management, support climate adaptation, and address carbon management to offset greenhouse gas emissions, while also benefiting both people and nature; see doi.gov/pressreleases/interior-department-announces-new-actions-support-nature-based-solutions (accessed April 10, 2024).

dikes, and bulkheads to wetlands, marshes, and dunes or a combination of both hard (gray) and soft (green) techniques in urban sites with limited space. The significance in scale and impact of these projects warrants the addition of a new layer to the preservation powers of the Landmarks Law that focuses on resiliency, biodiversity, and connectivity. While many of these sites are already protected by federal and state designations, they are noticeably absent from the Landmarks Map of the city. If landmark designation is considered a value statement of what we wish to preserve, then New York City landmarks need to be expanded to include the protection and care of our environment.

AN ECOLOGICAL WORLDVIEW

The public realm presents an opportunity to promote a new set of values that prioritize people, foster environmental care and repair, and acknowledge and recognize the vital role that public spaces have in the city. It is time for us to change our approach from being defensive and reactive to being proactive and offensive. The Landmarks Law was initially created to protect historically significant buildings from being lost, but it needs to evolve to help us shape the city we desire. As New York City continues to move toward being more environmentally and ecologically focused, with equity at its core, the Landmarks Law needs to follow suit. It can become a proactive response to protecting, enhancing, and connecting natural and cultural landscapes that contribute to both the city's preservation and its growth.

Toward this end, I propose the following:

First, a landscape architect should be required to sit on the Landmarks Preservation Commission. The enabling legislation of the Commission reads: "The membership of such commission shall include at least three architects, one historian qualified in the field, one city planner or landscape architect, and one realtor." As indicated in the text, the landscape architect position is optional, and can be replaced by a city planner. Having a landscape architect as an ongoing part of the Landmarks Preservation Commission will expand the agency's expertise and provide a more holistic approach to decision-making.

Second, we should expand our criteria for designation, to be rooted in the city's diverse culture and with a renewed focus on the public realm and the environment. This expansion would involve revising current classifications for outdoor sites and considering the addition of a new classification, suggested here as "living landmarks." The term "living landmarks" is meant to capture the essential role of public spaces in our daily lives and the living natural world. This new designation would encompass an expanded public realm, including public streets, active neighborhood parks, cultural landscapes, and infrastructure reuse projects, as well as park districts, connective corridors, ecological landscapes, and comprehensive resiliency projects. The items underlined below identify potential revisions in the current language and the addition of a new category.

To become a scenic landmark, an outdoor site must:

- Be at least thirty years old
- Have "a special character or special historical, ecological, or aesthetic interest or value as part of the development, heritage, or cultural characteristics of the City, state, or nation"
- Be a landscape feature or aggregate of landscape features
- Contribute to increasing connectivity, access, and equity in the city

To become a historic district, the proposed collection of buildings must:

- Represent at least one period or style of architecture typical of one or more eras in the city's history
- Have a distinct "sense of place"
- Have a coherent streetscape that supports community

To become a living landmark, the proposed public street, infrastructure reuse project, cultural landscape, neighborhood park, park district, ecological landscape, or resiliency project must:

- Have significant scale, impact, and connectivity that increases habitat, biodiversity, and environmental resilience

- Have cultural significance in terms of its heritage, customs, use, and programming that promotes community cohesion, diversity, cultural identity, and social resilience
- Contribute to increasing connectivity, access, and equity in the city

As the Landmarks Law continues to establish the value of a place through designation based on historical, aesthetic, and cultural significance, it is crucial to consider how these values should evolve and reflect the New York City of today and tomorrow. By honoring current landmarks and designating new ones, we can find significance and a distinct sense of place that defines a new New York and fosters the long-term care of our land and water. A landscape approach allows us to reimagine our public spaces, to enhance and prioritize both the human experience and our environment in a city that is constantly evolving and striving to do and be better. Consider my argument a call to action, to preserve and safeguard the public realm and move beyond the scenic, toward an ecological worldview. 🏛

The Greek sculptor Eutychides created a statue of Tyche of Antioch slightly after 300 BCE. For the next five hundred years, artists copied the statue in a variety of scales and materials. In this copy, she holds in her right hand a sheaf of grain, a symbol of prosperity. Wrapped in long garments, she wears a crown in the form of city walls. PHOTO: ALAMY.

ADAM GOPNIK

A TRACT FOR TYCHE:
OR, WHAT TO DO ABOUT THE BROWNSTONES AND THE BOOKSTORES

ALTHOUGH ATHENA IS, by usual account, the patron goddess of the Greek city, she's a busy woman, given everything else she had to tend to – wisdom, olives, owls, all of that . . . so in truth the ancients surrendered the special care of cities to a secondary goddess, less capacious but more single-mindedly devoted. Tyche is that girl, the patroness of cities who doubled, tellingly, as the goddess of luck – indeed, a later Roman avatar of Tyche, as Fortuna, still presides over the most beautiful of cities, Venice, twirling, "in rotary bronze loveliness," as Henry James put it, above the Dogana. She is associated especially with the great cosmopolitan cities of antiquity, Alexandria above all, where her sanctuary was said to be particularly beautiful.

What better goddess to appeal to, then, for the well-being of New York? A city of luck and fortune, good and bad alike, and the inheritor, surely, of those cosmopolitan cities of antiquity. Yet in the past half-century, Tyche has been twirling with particular violence above our town, turning from one vision of the city to another. For those of us who are neither architectural historians nor "critics" nor experts of any kind, but only city dwellers who love cities to the exclusion of all other arrangements, still have enough consciousness to know that we have lived, in one lifetime, through two revolutions in the way we think about urban life.

The first, now more than half a century old, was the Jane Jacobs revolution, when that saintly figure asked us to see aged and ordinary city blocks, not in the horrible Corbusian model as dated contrivances, nor as mere slums to be swept away, but as intricately wrought, living systems – as ecologically balanced and self-emerging as any coral reef. The life of the street was identical to the life of the city. Instead of solving scale by building big, we learned that small, habitable streets with discernible horizons were not cosmetic but essential – that without them New York was brain dead, if you will, since the city's streets were its neurons. The fundamental task of architecture and urbanism was then to preserve and renew, not to destroy and rebuild.

The virtues of this mixed-use, old-fashioned street-corner urbanism went far past mere pleasure: in the fight against crime, a Korean deli open all night in mid-block was more valuable than any cop car, and in the remaking of neighborhoods, every 6-story building was far more valuable – and desirable – than its neighboring modern high-rise. Small shops, rehabilitated spaces... the residential resettling of whole areas of the city – from SoHo to Williamsburg – owed most, explicitly and by common feeling, to this understanding. Instead of razing, rehabilitate; instead of thinking big – think small, and the results will be, emotionally, big. This was the sensibility under whose star all of us who made New York our homes in the 1980s and 1990s resided, and it led to neighborhood salvation and to the feeling that every brownstone saved from the wrecker's ball was a bit of the city's intelligence saved from a lobotomy.

But now we are living through a counterrevolution, not yet always as evident, but every bit as real. It is the movement, sometimes called by the acronym YIMBY – Yes, In My Backyard, to distinguish it from an earlier insistent No! to development – that seeks to share good fortune, maintain a large and varied population of classes and kinds, and does this above all by choosing to build. Its central thesis is simple: the solution to the housing crisis is housing. We cannot afford not to. The Jacobite city is quaint and lovable, but impossible to sustain – all that happens when we try to sustain it is to turn it into a dainty museum of itself, a kind of permanent Petit Trianon,

General Motors Headquarters (1968), 432 Park Avenue (2015), and the Sherry Netherland Hotel (1927)—a cluster of buildings that evokes the layers of architectural history visible throughout New York City. PHOTO: ZACK DEZON.

where upper-middle-class people get to play at being urban dwellers as Marie Antoinette's ladies got to play at being milkmaids.

I first became aware of the potential power of this reevaluation in reading, and then writing about, Lizabeth Cohen's provocative – an overused word, but appropriate here – life of Ed Logue, long the Lex Luthor of Jane Jacobs's version of Metropolis. The spirit of Logue had clearly been summoned in response to the current crisis of the American city: the crisis of affordable housing, and, with it, the disaster of cities being made monocultural by their success. The sign of the city, after all, seems less visible in revived streets than in the new generation of residential towers, rising in their vertiginous narrowness and affordable to only the elect; the symbols of our time: the wealthy giving the finger to the city. The Oligarchs' Erections, I have called these thin and obnoxious towers – but they are as much the visual symbol of New York now as the great 1930s skyscrapers were the symbols of a romantic view of American industry, or as the great buildings of Riverside Drive were of middle-class New York in its ascendancy. (My great-aunt, who worked as a translator at the U.N., lived in a ten-room apartment at 115th and Riverside, but abandoned it in the 1980s, during the worst of the crime wave.) We suffer these days from urban diseases of affluence – too much money chasing too little land – but we should remember what diseases of privation were like.

The YIMBY movement insists on the proposition that the way forward for New York – Manhattan in particular – is to build. Build and build more. In a conversation at the height of the pandemic, the NYU (and Paris-raised) urbanist Alain Bertaud told me that "the idea that Manhattan is too dense is *absurd*. The population of Manhattan was nearly double what it is now eighty years ago. Strangely enough, the decrease in population in Paris and Manhattan are absolutely parallel. What can we do? We have to remove the regulatory constraints. The NIMBY phenomenon is out of hand. You want to build a bakery? You're told you can't have a bakery here – a hardware store but not a bakery." He pointed out a range of local initiatives where developers – he indicated particularly a tower on Amsterdam Avenue – which, though completely legal, were subject to a neighborhood group suing, "saying it was not in the character of the neighborhood – a neighborhood full of towers! – and the judge asked the developer to remove twenty stories. So, this is of course terrible – instead of housing affordability it means that only very expensive buildings can be built. So, you need even more lawyers – in order for your building to survive." (The developers of 200 Amsterdam, to be sure, after much litigation got to build to their original plan.) He calls this the "Double Whammy" of New York – too much regulation and too much local control, leaving us with an underpopulated city – and this at a time when the people who make New York work, from schoolteachers to police officers, often have a two-hour commute into a city they can no longer afford to live in. Regulation established in the 1960s turned, he points out, "on the idea that the Seagram's Building was an example of good urban design – even though it was very expensive – and so the idea of the planners became not to mix externalities but to promote good design. But you can't promote good design through regulations – the Seagram's Building was built by a wealthy family." The oligarch's erection, far from being a new thing, is, in effect, a New York building type.

Developers good; local residents bad. A shocking thought for people committed to urbanism, and yet now contagious. If we accept the thicket of local authorities that disable new development, we are actually, in the long run, damaging the most powerless people in the city, and accommodating the most affluent. The desire to keep neighborhoods intact means keeping them intact for me, and mine, not for yours, much less everyone.

Yet here – Tyche twists again in the wind – a new problem arises to the eye of the city lover. For though the problem of building new housing is usually discussed in terms of plans and zones and taxes, it is also – no, it is above all – an aesthetic and architectural one. The YIMBY movement – I look at one of my favorite morning "reads," Matthew Yglesias, as an instance – tends to treat the architectural issues as secondary or, most often, merely "ornamental" or cosmetic. The necessary corrective to unrestrained Jacobite-ism threatens a new Philistinism of its own – one in which the essential lessons painfully learned over the years, which cost us Penn Station and nearly cost us an expressway through what's now SoHo – where building is paramount and how the city is going to look and feel becomes a Christmas-wrapping problem. When we ask ourselves what pains us in the city, we think of losses. We think of bookstores now turned into banks. We think of brownstones now demolished and transformed into high-rises. All the cries about population density and the necessity of development cannot console us for their loss. Bookstores and brownstones are what we mean by the city, and when we lose them, we lose it.

Yet, since the time of Jacobs – indeed, for that matter, since the time of John Ruskin, in the mid-nineteenth century – a central lesson in thinking about building is to think about buildings. The small stuff – style, scale, façade, signs of life, the richness of decorative detail, variety rather than uniformity, the encrustations of ornament – counts big. Putting up tall buildings in the West Village is one way to get more supply to meet the demand, but the demand in this case – or, at least, the acceptance of new buildings by local incumbents – will alter as the supply becomes unappealing. It is not location alone that makes such neighborhoods attractive, but what is *local* about the location, its particular spell of kinds and purposes and incomes. If people thought that the new buildings going up in cities would be appealing to live in, they would not protest new buildings in advance. If we knew how to make new buildings better, we would accept new buildings more.

The practical ins and outs – where money is to be made, there buildings will be found; how developers can be made more prodigal without becoming more predatory – raise questions that the inexpert eye of the essayist can only guess at. But perhaps it is time for a rejuvenated Jacobite manifesto – or kind of an enforceable Constitution rather than the compact of ideas and emotions and exhortations that have to serve us instead. Let us call it a Tractate for Tyche, a series of commitments we make to ourselves and to her. One announcing a few of what should be accepted premises – not axioms, which are unchanging, but pragmatic principles, capable of being adapted.

1. Cities are organic, self-emerging places. Trying to "God" them is a permanent error. Large-scale projects rarely work; small-scale adjustments do.

2. High-density, small-scale, mixed-use streets before blocks, and blocks before big development — these remain ideals worth asserting and searching for.

3. There are never too many parks for people.

4. Cities can thrive with almost any amount of inconvenience, over-abundance, even ugliness. What they cannot survive is the bleak ugliness of depopulation. Every espresso bar that opens is a gift from the god of cities.

5. The cosmetic aspect of cities and the functional aspect of cities are part of a single plan — of a single discourse, as the French would say. To be indifferent to the sheer look of things — their scale, their place-ment, their contiguity — is to refuse to learn the lessons that history has so laboriously tried to teach us. Salvation will not lie in simple overbuilding.

6. But, as we have also learned, the effort to preserve cities leads us too neatly exactly to the "Venetian temptation" — where a preservative becomes a paralytic, and over time what were once mixed neighbor-hoods become the preserves of the very wealthy. (And then over time, as in London, become the preserves of the ghosts, the nonresidents.)

7. There never need be — nor is there in truth — a "trade-off" between aesthetic values and architectural progress. The right solutions will be pleasing to the senses as they are sensible to the city.

And here, perhaps, we end with the great mystery of cities now. Why is there no readily turned-to model of what humane, high-density, inclusive urban housing would look like? Or, rather, the problem is that we *do* know

Brownstones in Harlem at Manhattan Avenue and West 122nd Street, 2018. PHOTO: BRAD DICKSON.

what humane, high-density, inclusive urban housing looks like. It looks like what we've got already and don't have enough to share. The trouble is not that we don't recognize it but that we can't reproduce it. Harlem has been expensively "reoccupied" by urban professionals because the streets and the housing stock of Harlem, paralyzed by prejudice for so long, are intrinsically appealing to anyone who has the chance to live there. It is not a taste for the retro, or mere nostalgia, that makes this happen. It is a recognition that the building habits of times past created spaces that are more hospitable than the sterility of time present.

How do we build on Jacobite principles to an expansive turn? An earnest search for award-winning, successful contemporary public-housing schemes turns up disappointingly little; they tend to be French, Spanish, or Slovenian, and, though they doubtless have many virtues, for the most part they do fall prey to the Jacobite sins of streetlessness and typically still take the form of towers in the middle of a plaza, albeit often more brightly colored or oddly shaped than their dynamited predecessors. *We're* not Corbusian nightmares, they seem to insist. We're *neighborhoods* – 30 stories high, on a plaza.

The magnetic appeal of the old "organic" cities, from the northern Italian hill towns to the center of Paris, remains overt testimony to the resistant truth: we know what makes cities work, but we can't seem to work them adequately. Alain Bertaud has also observed, in reference to housing policies, that, while the law of supply and demand may be as fixed as the law of gravity, well, we defy the law of gravity all the time. We build balloons and airplanes and elevators to counter it. What we can't do is *repeal* the law of gravity – take an ordinary rug and declare that it's a magic carpet. Some city planning is like the crafting of an airplane, or at least an elevator: we can protect small merchants with ordinances that limit the size of their competitors, as happens in France, or with tax structures that would discourage landlords from maintaining empty storefronts while holding out for national chains that could pay the exorbitant rents they hope for, rather than continuing to accept lower rents actually available from the bookstore or the wine shop. We can insist (as we're already beginning to do) on social housing as part of every development. Other projects, like rent control, are clearly magic carpets that won't fly with the best intentions in the world; all rent control does is to reward the incumbents and punish the incomers. We can continue to defy the law of gravity, with Tyche's blessing, but we can do so only if we recognize the truth that cities are as many canvases for artists as they are tracts for developers, and that the small, ornamental, cosmetic, intricate choices we make are disproportionately responsible for the feelings that the city can still excite in us. Asked to choose between Jerusalem and Athens – between the city of faith and the city of reason – New Yorkers have a simple answer: take Alexandria, the cosmopolitan city of choices. It's Tyche's town.

Manhattanhenge Sunrise. This annual celestial show occurs when the rising and setting sun aligns perfectly with the Manhattan street grid. PHOTO: GARY HERSHORN/GETTY IMAGES.

CONTRIBUTORS

BARBARALEE DIAMONSTEIN-SPIELVOGEL has been a leading voice during the last sixty years on some of the defining urban issues of our time. As a White House Assistant, she created the first and only White House Festival of the Arts (1965) and helped create the White House Fellows and the Presidential Scholars Programs. As the first director of New York City's newly created Department of Cultural Affairs (1966), she brought the first public art exhibit to Bryant Park, the first public performance by the Metropolitan Opera to Central Park, and the first weeklong festival of films about New York to The Regency Theater.

She was appointed to the board of the U.S. Holocaust Memorial Museum by President Reagan (1987), and named chair of the committee that commissioned art for all of the museum's public spaces. President Clinton appointed her to the U.S. Commission of Fine Arts (1996), where she was the first woman in its then 109-year history to be elected vice chair (2002). As President Obama's appointee (2009–2018), she served on the American Battle Monuments Commission, and was named chair of their New Monuments Committee. In 2022, President Biden appointed her to the President's Advisory Committee on the Arts.

The longest-serving commissioner of the New York City Landmarks Preservation Commission (1972–1987), and chair of the New York City

Landmarks Preservation Foundation (1987–1995), she created and commissioned the now-standard Street Name signs and Markers/Maps programs, which identify all of New York City's historic districts. As chair of the Historic Landmarks Preservation Center since 1995, she created the Cultural Medallions program to commemorate notable New Yorkers (145 have been placed, located in all five boroughs). In 2007, she was appointed to the New York State Council on the Arts (NYSCA), where she was vice chair, and from 2016 to 2018 was NYSCA chair and CEO. And in 2023, she was appointed by New York Governor Hochul to the City University of New York (CUNY) board of trustees.

The recipient of four honorary doctorates (The Maryland Institute of Art, 1990; Longwood University, Virginia, 1996; Pratt Institute, Brooklyn, 2011; and Purchase College, State University of New York, 2017), numerous honors and awards—including her election as an honorary member of the AIA at the 2005 Annual Meeting of the American Institute of Architects—and with service to many boards, Diamonstein-Spielvogel earned her doctorate with high honors from New York University. A long-term board member of PEN America, she was also elected an honorary member of PEN Slovakia. She is a recipient of the Dr. Ján Papánek Medal, one of the highest honors accorded by the Slovak Republic, awarded for significant contributions in promoting values of freedom, democracy, and human rights as well as the values and principles of the United Nations. She has shared her scholarship through twenty-four books about art, architecture, photography, crafts, design, and public policy; numerous museum exhibitions; and as a television interviewer and producer for local and national networks such as A&E, CBS, and NBC. Her book *Handmade in America* was the basis of the first exhibition of crafts in the White House; her *Landmarks of New York* inspired an exhibition that toured with the U.S. Department of State to eighty-two countries on five continents, with ancillary activities (many led by Diamonstein-Spielvogel).

VISHAAN CHAKRABARTI is the founder and creative director of Practice for Architecture and Urbanism | PAU. As director of the Department of City Planning's Manhattan Office during the Bloomberg administration, he collaborated on efforts to save the High Line, extend the #7 subway line, rebuild the East River Waterfront, and restore the World Trade Center site after 9/11. The author of *A Country of Cities: A Manifesto for an Urban America* (Metropolis Books, 2013) and *The Architecture of Urbanity: Designing Cities for Pluralism and Planet* (Princeton University Press, 2024), he taught at Columbia University's Graduate School of Architecture, Planning and Preservation from 2009 to 2019, first as Marc Holliday Professor and Director of the MS in Real Estate Development, and then, in 2011, as the founding director of the Center for Urban Real Estate. From 2020 to 2021 he was the William W. Wurster Dean of the College of Environmental Design at the University of California, Berkeley, and now serves on the boards of the Architectural League of New York, the Regional Plan Association, the Norman Foster Foundation, The World Around, and Prometheus Materials.

JUSTIN DAVIDSON has been the architecture and classical music critic at *New York* magazine since 2007; his architecture columns also appear on the magazine's website *Curbed*. A native of Rome, he began his journalism career as a local stringer for the Associated Press in Rome. He worked as editorial director at Sony Classical before joining *Newsday*, where he spent twelve years as their classical music critic. Davidson won a Pulitzer Prize for Criticism in 2002 and was a finalist again in 2020. He has contributed to many publications, including *The New Yorker* and the *New York Review of Books*. The author of *Magnetic City: A Walking Companion to New York* (2017), he is an adjunct associate professor at Columbia University's Graduate School of Architecture, Planning and Preservation.

ANDREW DOLKART is a professor of historic preservation at Columbia University's Graduate School of Architecture, Planning and Preservation, and cofounder and codirector of the NYC LGBT Historic Sites Project. The author of *Morningside Heights: A History of Its Architecture and Development* (1998), which received the Association of American Publishers' award for best scholarly book in architecture and urban design, and *The Row House Reborn: Architecture and Neighborhoods in New York City, 1908–1929* (2009), which won the Society of Architectural Historians' Antoinette Forrester Downing Book Award, he is the recipient of the Historic Districts Council's Landmarks Lion Award and the New York Landmarks Conservancy's Lucy G. Moses Preservation Leadership Award.

THOMAS DYJA is the author of *New York, New York, New York: Four Decades of Success, Excess, and Transformation* (2021) and *The Third Coast: When Chicago Built the American Dream* (2013), winner of the *Chicago Tribune*'s 2013 Heartland Prize for Non-fiction; both were New York Times Notable books. Along with three novels and a biography of civil rights leader Walter White, he has written for *The New York Times*, the *Wall Street Journal*, and the *Architectural Record*. He is currently working on a history of clothing in New York City.

PAUL GOLDBERGER, a leading figure in architecture criticism, began his career at *The New York Times*, where, in 1984, his architecture criticism was awarded the Pulitzer Prize for Criticism. From 1997 to 2011, he served as the architecture critic for *The New Yorker*. He is the author of numerous books, including *ALLPARK: Baseball in the American City* (2019); *Building Art: The Life and Work of Frank Gehry* (2015); *Why Architecture Matters* (2009); and *DUMBO: The Making of a Neighborhood* (2021). He holds the Joseph Urban Chair in Design and Architecture at The New School, and was formerly dean of the Parsons School of Design. In 2012, he received the Vincent Scully Prize from the National Building Museum, and in 2017 he received the Award in Architecture from the American Academy of Arts and Letters. He is currently a contributing editor at *Vanity Fair*.

ADAM GOPNIK has been a staff writer for *The New Yorker* since 1986. He served as the magazine's art critic from 1987 to 1995 and their Paris correspondent from 1995 to 2000. He has been a contributor to numerous anthologies; his books include *Paris to the Moon* (2000), *The Table Comes First: Family, France, and The Meaning of Food* (2011), *A Thousand Small Sanities: The Moral Adventure of Liberalism* (2019), and *So Many Steves* (2023). Gopnik lectures widely and has won three National Magazine Awards for essays and for criticism (1997, 2001, 2005), and the George Polk Award for Magazine Reporting (1997). In March 2013, he was awarded the medal of Chevalier of the Order of Arts and Letters, and, in 2021, was made an *officier* of the Legion d'Honneur, France's highest military or civilian decoration.

MICHAEL KIMMELMAN has been the architecture critic of *The New York Times* since 2011, and is the author of *Portraits: Talking with Artists at the Met, the Modern, the Louvre, and Elsewhere* (1998), *The Accidental Masterpiece: On the Art of Life and Vice Versa* (2005), and *The Intimate City: Walking New York* (2022). An adjunct professor at Columbia University's Graduate School of Architecture, Planning and Preservation, he was previously *The New York Times* chief art critic and the creator of the "Abroad" column, covering significant global issues. Twice a finalist for the Pulitzer Prize, he is a regular contributor to the *New York Review of Books* and delivered the Robert B. Silvers Lecture at the New York Public Library (2005). He is also the recipient of numerous honors, including the Brendan Gill Prize (2014), and doctorates from The Corcoran School of the Arts and Design (2013) and the Pratt Institute (2014).

GUY NORDENSON is a structural engineer and professor of architecture and structural engineering at Princeton University. His projects include the Santa Fe Opera House, the Toledo Glass Pavilion, the National Museum of African American History and Culture, Washington, D.C., and the International African American Museum and Emmanuel Nine Memorial in Charleston, South Carolina. Nordenson's decades-long relationship with the

Museum of Modern Art includes cocurating the 2004 exhibition "Tall Buildings," and the publications *Tall Buildings* (MoMA, 2004); *Seven Structural Engineers: The Felix Candela Lectures* (MoMA, 2008); and *Structured Lineages: Learning from Japanese Structural Design* (MoMA, 2019). A former member of the New York City Public Design Commission and the New York City Panel on Climate Change, he is a member of the American Academy of Arts and Sciences and the National Academy of Engineering.

NAT OPPENHEIMER joined Silman, a TYLin Company, in 1988, and is principal in charge. His many projects include the new Whitney Museum in New York City and the National Museum of African American History and Culture, Washington, D.C. A board member of the Architectural League of New York and the Van Alen Institute International Council, Nat is a visiting lecturer at the Graduate School of Architecture, Princeton University, and has taught at Columbia University's Graduate School of Architecture, Planning and Preservation; Parsons; and the New School for Design. He is a member of the Grace Farms Foundation Architecture + Construction Working Group, which advocates to end the use of modern slavery in materials and labor for the built environment.

A. O. SCOTT was the cochief film critic at *The New York Times* from January 2000 until 2023, when he joined the Times Book Review as a critic at large, contributing essays and reviews on literature, culture, and society. After starting his career at *The New York Review of Books*, he then served as book critic for *Newsday*, while contributing to *Slate*, *The Atlantic*, and other publications. He is the author of *Better Living through Criticism: How to Think about Art, Pleasure, Beauty, and Truth* (2016). Distinguished professor of film criticism at Wesleyan University, in his spare time he plays mandolin, twelve-string guitar, and mountain dulcimer in the Loose Cannon Jug Band, an old-timey combo based in Surry, Maine.

LISA SWITKIN, partner at Field Operations, has a background in urban planning and landscape architecture and has been involved in numerous multidisciplinary projects, including New York City's High Line, Domino Park in Brooklyn, Santa Monica's Tongva Park, Gansevoort Peninsula in Hudson River Park, the 520-acre Sojourner Truth State Park in the Hudson Valley, the transformative master plan for Staten Island's Freshkills Park, and, recently, Cleveland's North Coast Lakefront. She was a Rome Prize recipient at the American Academy in Rome in 2008, and is past president of the Landscape Architecture Foundation. Lisa currently sits on the board of the Urban Design Forum. A registered landscape architect in New York, she has taught graduate-level design studios and lectured at Harvard University, the University of Pennsylvania, New York Botanical Gardens, and other universities, symposia, and institutions around the world.

ROSEMARY VIETOR, a fifteenth-generation Bowne family member, is vice president of the Bowne House Historical Society; the Society operates the 1661 Bowne House, the oldest surviving structure in Flushing, Queens. A New York City and National Landmark, Bowne House was recently recognized by the U.S. National Park Service as a member of its National Underground Railroad Network to Freedom program. Vietor is also a trustee of the New York State Archives Partnership Trust in Albany, and formerly served on the Board of the Colonial Dames of America. After a distinguished career as an executive in finance, Vietor became involved with preservation issues; she served on the local historical commission, the town historical society, and spearheaded the designation of a historic district in Sharon, Connecticut.

Photo editor **SARA BARRETT** is senior photo editor at *The New York Times*. Prior to joining the paper, she oversaw the photojournalism program at Columbia University, where she also taught photography for many years. In her first years in New York, she worked as a freelance photographer and photo editor. Her photographs have appeared in *The New Yorker*, *Vanity Fair*, *Esquire*, *The Times*, and a number of other publications, including *Spy*, where she was one of the original contributors.

Mapmaker **LARRY BUCHANAN** works at the intersection of art and journalism. A writer and artist, and the recipient of two Emmy Awards, he has spent more than a decade at *The New York Times*, where he is graphic editor, covering stories in almost every area. Much of his work focuses on using a variety of visual forms—maps, charts, diagrams, photographs, video—to explain the world. Clarity is the guiding principle of his work.

ACKNOWLEDGMENTS

TO THE OWNERS, OCCUPANTS, and managing agents of landmark buildings, concerned citizens, architects, engineers, landscape architects, preservationists, historians, and the wide range of individual and institutional resources that are involved with and support New York City's landmarks, history, and cultural heritage, my special thanks.

And to the organizations that make up the NYC Landmarks60 Alliance, a consortium of individuals and groups who have come together since 2012 to ensure that the NYC Landmarks Law continues to preserve our architectural heritage and to foster the next generation of historic preservationists. Particular thanks, as well, to all those who have joined or will join us to help commemorate 2025—the celebration of the 60th Anniversary of the passage of the NYC Landmarks Law.

A special tribute to:

Sara Barrett, photography editor, whose expertise and discerning eye add visual excitement to each essay.

Larry Buchanan, Josh Katz, Rumsey Taylor, and Eve Washington, the creators of "An Extremely Detailed Map of New York City Neighborhoods," from *The New York Times* (October 29, 2023), for their inspired maps, created for *The New York Times,* and adopted, with their permission, to underscore and reinforce some ideas in this book.

ACKNOWLEDGMENTS

And, all thanks to:

Deborah Bershad Addeo, whose intelligent views and expert skills have helped bring this thoughtful publication to fruition.

Kathryn O. Greenberg, for her deep understanding and regard for the creative process.

And to Harrison Carter for his informed taste, measured restraint, and collaborative spirit.

To our publisher, Rea Hederman, at New York Review Books.

And to Raquel Valencia, for her very helpful assistance, as well.